A2

English *for* EMAILS

SHORT COURSE SERIES

Rebecca Turner

Impressum

Verfasser:	Rebecca Turner
Berater:	Katherine Jähnig, Berlin
	Louise Kennedy, Hamburg
Projektleitung:	Andreas Göbel
Redaktion:	Anna Batrla, Meike Kolle
Außenredaktion:	Janan Barksdale, Berlin
Bildredaktion:	Janan Barksdale, Berlin
Redaktionelle Mitarbeit:	Christine House, Rani Kumar, Zsuzsa Parádi
Layoutkonzept:	finedesign, Berlin
Technische Umsetzung:	zweiband.media, Berlin
Umschlagsgestaltung:	Studio SYBERG, Berlin; Jan Haux / Pepe Jürgens, Berlin

Quellen

Titelfoto © Fotolia, lichtmeister | S. 4 v.o.: © Fotolia, MH; © Shutterstock, 3Dstock; © Fotolia, ra2studio; © Shutterstock, Zygotehaasnobrain; © Shutterstock, Mmaxer | S. 5 © Shutterstock, vinnstock; © Shutterstock, Leonardo da; © Shutterstock, Diego Cervo | S. 6 © Fotolia, MH | S. 7 © Shutterstock, WavebreakMedia | S. 12 © Shutterstock, 3Dstock | S. 17 © Shutterstock, spaxiax | S. 18 © Fotolia, ra2studio | S. 21 © Shutterstock, Syda Productions | S. 24 v.o.: © Shutterstock, Zygotehaasnobrain; © Shutterstock, lightwavemedia | S. 25 © Shutterstock, lightwavemedia | S. 29 © Shutterstock, sarahdesign | S. 30 v.o.: © Shutterstock, Mmaxer; © Shutterstock, wavebreakmedia | S. 32 © Shutterstock, wavebreakmedia | S. 36 © Shutterstock, vinnstock | S. 37 © Fotolia, Janina Dierks | S. 39 © Shutterstock, Monkey Business Images | S. 41 © Shutterstock, stockyimages | S. 42 © vShutterstock, Leonardo da | S. 44 © Shutterstock, Ron Dale | S. 45 © Shutterstock, racorn | S. 46 v.o.: © Shutterstock, wavebreakmedia; © Shutterstock, Ersler Dmitry | S. 47 © Shutterstock, Diego Cervo | S. 50 © Shutterstock, Carsten Reisinger

www.cornelsen.de

1. Auflage, 1. Druck 2016

Alle Drucke dieser Auflage sind inhaltlich unverändert und können im Unterricht nebeneinander verwendet werden.

© 2016 Cornelsen Schulverlage GmbH, Berlin

Druck: Mohn Media Mohndruck, Gütersloh

ISBN 978-3-464-20575-4

PEFC zertifiziert
Dieses Produkt stammt aus nachhaltig bewirtschafteten Wäldern und kontrollierten Quellen.
www.pefc.de

English for Emails im Überblick

Willkommen zu Ihrem A2 Short Course *English for Emails*. Mit diesem Buch möchten wir Ihnen das Werkzeug und Know-how vermitteln, englischsprachige E-Mails von Begrüßung bis Abschluss strukturiert zu schreiben. Dabei geht es uns vor allem um die vielen unterschiedlichen Arten von Geschäfts-E-Mails, die in der globalen Welt immer wieder geschrieben werden müssen. In acht Units entwickeln Sie die Fertigkeit und das notwendige Vokabular, um mit solch relevanten Themen wie bspw. Anfragen schicken, Fristen setzen oder Termine vereinbaren umzugehen.

- Die acht Units bringen Ihnen Schritt für Schritt auf jeweils sechs Seiten das wichtigste Vokabular und grundlegende Formulierungen näher.

- Anhand von realistischen Kommunikationsszenarien aus dem geschäftlichen E-Mail-Alltag festigen vielfältige Übungen das gelernte Wissen. Sie werden von Mal zu Mal sicherer im Verfassen englischer E-Mails an Kollegen oder Geschäftspartner..

- Die für E-Mails wichtigsten Formulierungen eignen Sie sich aktiv mithilfe der *Phrase boxes* an und können diese am Ende jeder Unit noch einmal in den *Key phrases* wiederholen.

- Mit *Over to you* baut das Buch auf Ihren vorhandenen Kenntnissen im Bereich geschäftlicher Kommunikation auf und fördert diese. Durch Partnerübungen werden Sie dazu animiert, eigene Erfahrungen auszutauschen.

- Jede Unit endet mit *Last but not least*, einem kurzem Text zum Thema, der ausgiebig zu Diskussionen einlädt.

- Authentische Dialoge auf der beiliegenden CD schulen Ihr Hörverstehen. Mit einer Reihe an Akzenten bereiten Sie sich darauf vor, Englisch auch über E-Mails hinaus zu begegnen.

- Im Anhang finden Sie zusätzlich einen Reihe von Beispiel-E-Mails, die Ihnen jederzeit einen Abgleich ermöglichen und als Formulierungshilfe dienen. Darüber hinaus sind dort eine umfassende Liste mit den wichtigsten Formulierungen, Transkripte für die Höraufgaben, einen Lösungsschlüssel und eine A-Z Wortliste.

Die Autorin und die Redaktion wünschen Ihnen viel Freude und Erfolg mit *English for Emails*! Wir hoffen, dass es Ihnen auf Ihrem Weg zum sicheren Verfassen englischer E-Mails einen gelungenen Beitrag leisten wird.

Inhaltsverzeichnis

6 Making arrangements

- Arranging an appointment
- Suggesting a time and place
- Accepting an invitation
- Declining an invitation
- Changing an appointment

Page 36

would you have time?
how about meeting? **convenient**
Tuesday at 2:00 something has
see you on Friday come up

7 Checking information

- Starting the email
- Checking and clarifying information
- Asking for confirmation
- Correcting and confirming information

Page 42

just wanted to clarify
a summary of our discussion
actually can you please check?
is that right? comments below

8 Dealing with problems

- Making a complaint
- Asking for action
- Apologizing
- Offering solutions

Page 48

disappointed
writing to complain
please accept our apologies
satisfactory **hope this helps**
solution **free of charge**

Anhang

Symbole und Abkürzungen

◁ 02 Tracknummer

    Partnerarbeit

AE   amerikanisches Englisch

BE   britisches Englisch

sb.   somebody (jemand)

sth.   something (etwas)

Learning objectives
• Dealing with emails
  Mit E-Mails umgehen
• Replying to emails
  E-Mails beantworten
• Starting and closing an email
  Eine E-Mail beginnen und enden

1 Getting started

1 Answer the questions for yourself, then compare your answers with a partner.

1 How often do you receive or send emails in English?
   ☐ every day   ☐ once a week   ☐ other ....

2 Who do you write emails in English to?
   ☐ customers   ☐ colleagues   ☐ other ....

3 What nationalities are the people you send English emails to or receive emails from?
   ☐ native English speakers ....
   ☐ other ....

4 What fields do these people work in?
   ☐ same as you   ☐ other ....

5 What is the reason for writing English emails?
   ☐ to ask for information   ☐ to give information   ☐ other ....

6 How do you prefer to contact the people you work with in English?

   ☐ phone, because ....

   ☐ email, because ....

   ☐ face-to-face meetings, because ....

   ☐ video conferences, because ....

   ☐ other (how? why?) ....

> **Vocabulary**
>
> colleague Kollege/Kollegin
> customer Kunde/Kundin
> field Bereich, Gebiet
> to receive bekommen

2 Look at the email screen opposite and match 1–8 to the words below.

| attachment ☐ | folders ☐ | inbox ☐ | sent ☐ |
| drafts ☐ | high priority ☐ | outbox ☐ | subject ☐ |

Now match a–g to the following.

| send & receive ☐ | cc ☐ | reply ☐ | forward ☐ |
| delete ☐ | print ☐ | reply all ☐ | |

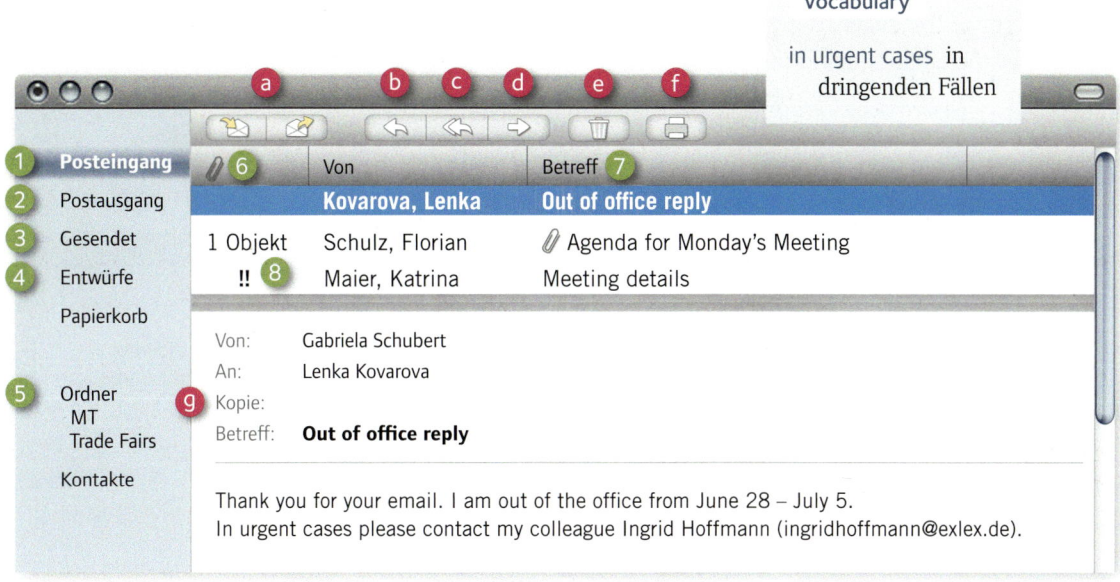

Vocabulary

in urgent cases in dringenden Fällen

---

3 ◁02 **Use words from exercise 2 to complete the sentences below. Then listen to check your answers.**

1 I've checked my .... and I have five new emails.

2 I'll .... your email to my colleague who is responsible for international orders.

3 I'm sending you our price list as an ....

4 Please .... Fritz and Sanjay so they also know about the changes.

5 This is an out of office message. I am on vacation until August 3 and will .... to your email when I return.

6 Please .... my last email. I sent you the wrong information.

Vocabulary

to be responsible for sth. für etw. zuständig sein
message Nachricht
vacation Urlaub

---

4 **Gabriela Schubert works in the marketing department at her company. She returns from her vacation and finds an inbox full of emails. What should she do with them? Match a subject line (a–f) to each action (1–6).**

Vocabulary

department Abteilung
minutes Protokoll
safety Sicherheits-

1 ▢ reply
2 ▢ forward
3 ▢ reply with attachment

4 ▢ delete
5 ▢ read, but don't reply
6 ▢ call

a   Subject: *SPAM* You have won a trip to Jamaica
b !! Subject: Safety training course – last chance!
c   Subject: Job in call center?
d   Subject: Minutes of meeting? Please send!
e   Subject: Out of office message
f   Subject: Present for Johanna's baby – ideas

👥 **Discuss with a partner.**
Do you have the same answers?

5 Look at four of the emails Gabriela received and match them to a subject line from exercise 4 (a–f). Are any of the emails similar to the ones you receive?

Email	1	2	3	4
Subject line				

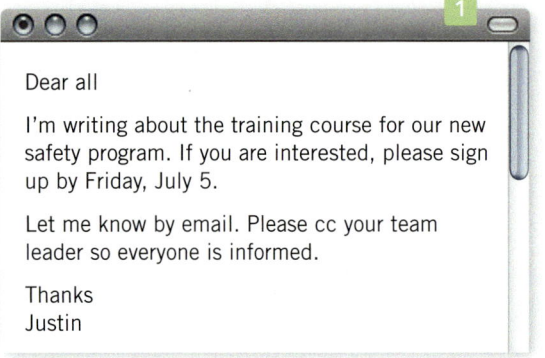

1

Dear all

I'm writing about the training course for our new safety program. If you are interested, please sign up by Friday, July 5.

Let me know by email. Please cc your team leader so everyone is informed.

Thanks
Justin

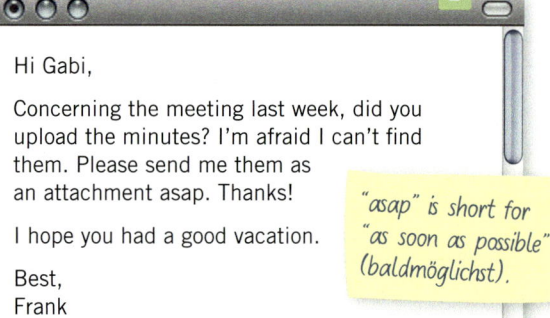

2

Hi Gabi,

Concerning the meeting last week, did you upload the minutes? I'm afraid I can't find them. Please send me them as an attachment asap. Thanks!

I hope you had a good vacation.

Best,
Frank

"asap" is short for "as soon as possible" (baldmöglichst).

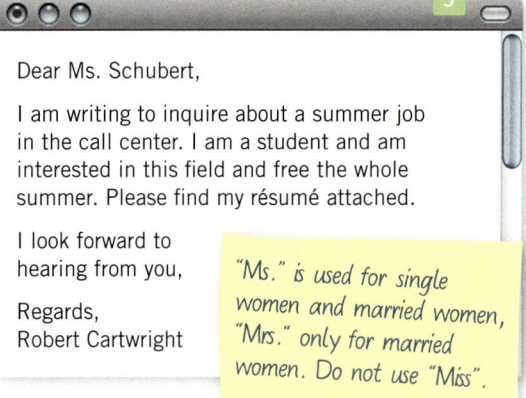

3

Dear Ms. Schubert,

I am writing to inquire about a summer job in the call center. I am a student and am interested in this field and free the whole summer. Please find my résumé attached.

I look forward to hearing from you,

Regards,
Robert Cartwright

"Ms." is used for single women and married women, "Mrs." only for married women. Do not use "Miss".

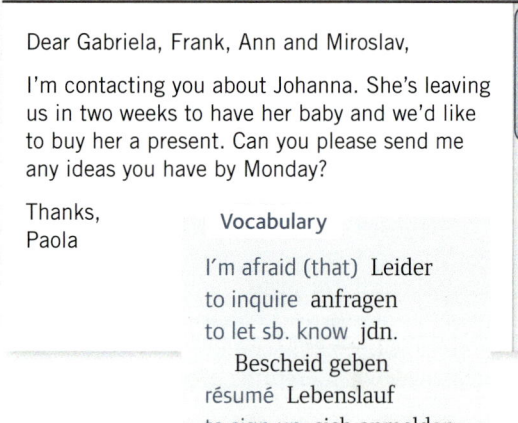

4

Dear Gabriela, Frank, Ann and Miroslav,

I'm contacting you about Johanna. She's leaving us in two weeks to have her baby and we'd like to buy her a present. Can you please send me any ideas you have by Monday?

Thanks,
Paola

Vocabulary

I'm afraid (that) Leider
to inquire anfragen
to let sb. know jdn. Bescheid geben
résumé Lebenslauf
to sign up sich anmelden

6 Look at the emails again and complete the phrases below.

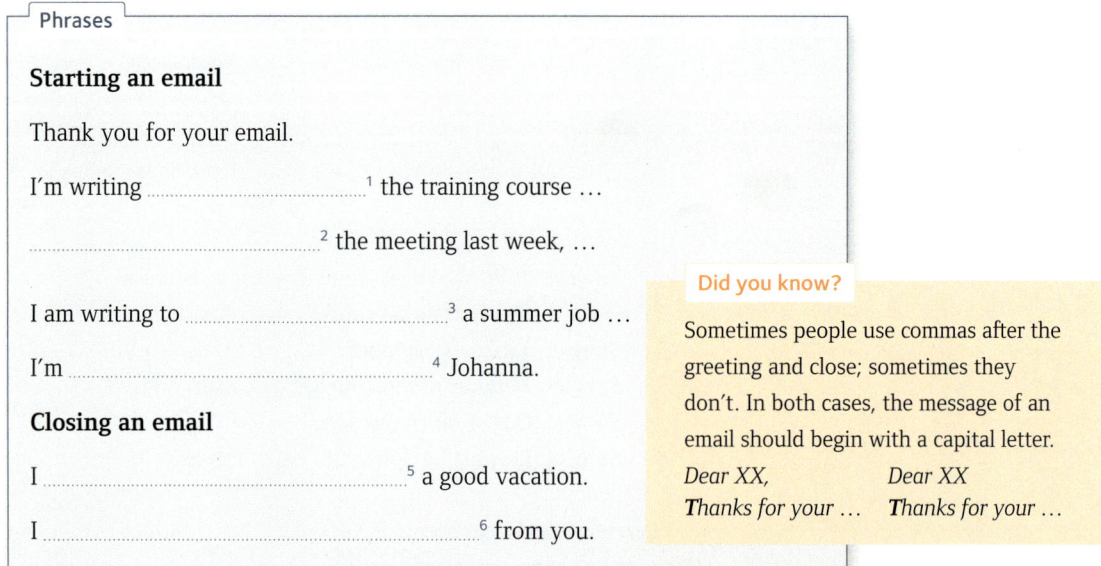

Phrases

Starting an email

Thank you for your email.

I'm writing ....¹ the training course …

................................² the meeting last week, …

I am writing to ....³ a summer job …

I'm ....⁴ Johanna.

Closing an email

I ....⁵ a good vacation.

I ....⁶ from you.

Did you know?

Sometimes people use commas after the greeting and close; sometimes they don't. In both cases, the message of an email should begin with a capital letter.

Dear XX,   *Dear XX*
Thanks for your …   *Thanks for your …*

7 Match the parts of the sentences.

1	I am writing	a	a good weekend.
2	I am contacting	b	the course, can we talk in the morning?
3	I hope you had	c	for your email.
4	Concerning	d	about the discussion we had yesterday.
5	I look forward	e	to your reply.
6	Thank you	f	you about the meeting.

8 ◁))03 Which email in exercise 5 do you think Gabriela replied to with a phone call? Listen to the conversation. Were you right? Why did she call?

After the phone call, Gabriela writes an email. Choose the correct phrases to complete the message.

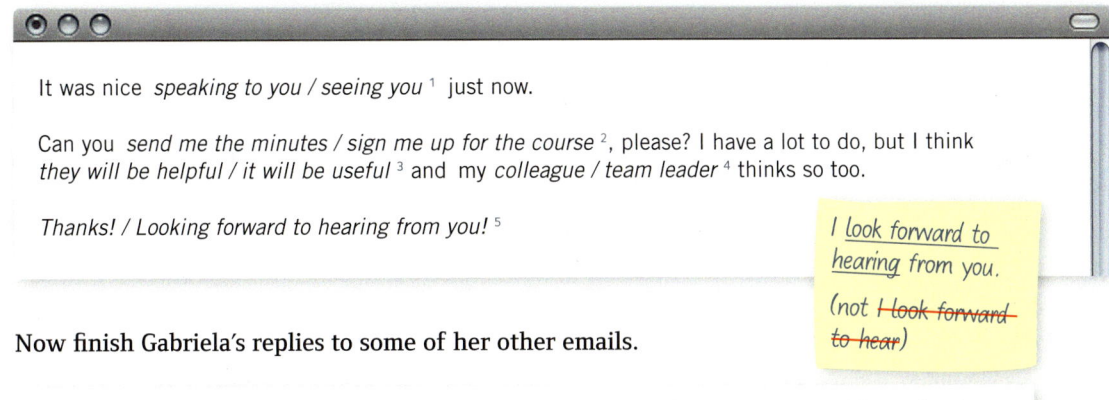

It was nice *speaking to you / seeing you* [1] just now.

Can you *send me the minutes / sign me up for the course* [2], please? I have a lot to do, but I think *they will be helpful / it will be useful* [3] and my *colleague / team leader* [4] thinks so too.

Thanks! / Looking forward to hearing from you! [5]

> I look forward to hearing from you. (not ~~I look forward to hear~~)

9 Now finish Gabriela's replies to some of her other emails.

attached · concerning · contacting · forwarding · let you know · responsible · thank you

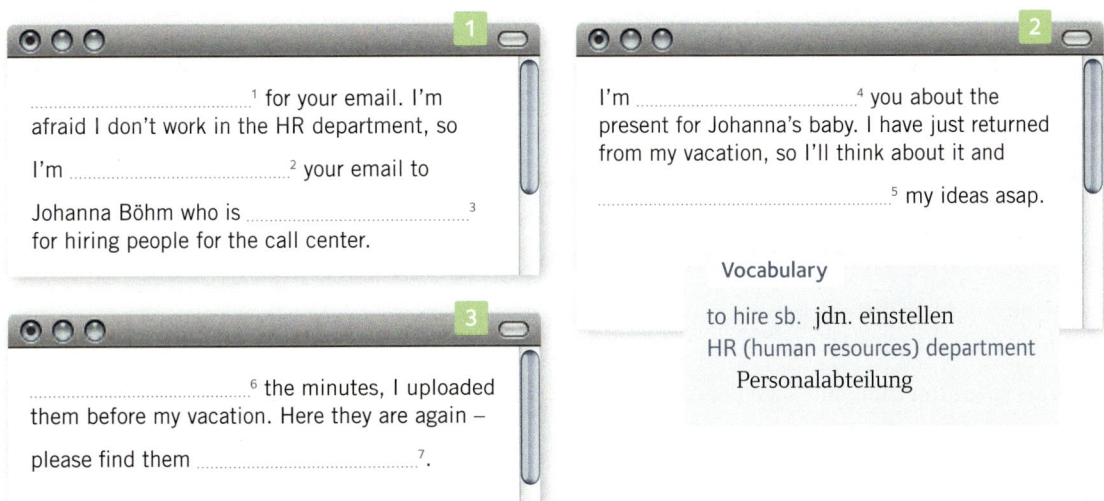

1

........................[1] for your email. I'm afraid I don't work in the HR department, so

I'm ....[2] your email to

Johanna Böhm who is ....[3] for hiring people for the call center.

2

I'm ....[4] you about the present for Johanna's baby. I have just returned from my vacation, so I'll think about it and

........................[5] my ideas asap.

Vocabulary

to hire sb. jdn. einstellen
HR (human resources) department Personalabteilung

3

........................[6] the minutes, I uploaded them before my vacation. Here they are again – please find them ....[7].

Match the greetings and closes below with the emails above. (Look back at exercise 5 if you need help.)

a	b	c	
Dear Paola	Hi Frank,	Dear Mr. Cartwright,	1 ▢
…	…	…	2 ▢
Regards	Best,	Best regards,	3 ▢
Gabriela	Gabi	Gabriela Schubert	

Here are some key phrases from the unit. Tick (✓) the ones that are useful for you.

Greetings
- Dear *(first name)*
- Dear Mr./Mrs./Ms. *(last name)*
- Dear all
- Dear Sam and Gina
- Hi/Hello *(first name)*

Starting an email
- Thank you for your email.
- It was nice speaking to / seeing you just now.
- I am writing about/concerning …
- I'm writing to ask/inquire about …
- I am contacting you about …
- Concerning the meeting / your question, …
- Please find … attached.
- I am forwarding your email to …

Starting and closing an email

Closing an email
- I hope you had a good vacation.
- Thanks.
- I look forward to hearing from you.
- Looking forward to your reply.

Two other typical closes are "All the best" and "Best wishes".

Closes
- Thanks
- Best
- Regards
- Best regards

What to do with an email: you can …
- send it
- send it high priority / as an urgent message
- receive it
- reply to it / answer it
- forward it to somebody
- attach a document to it
- print it

You will find an English–German list of these phrases on page 68.

Use this space to write your own useful words and phrases.

....

....

....

....

....

....

Over to you

10 Choose a person you regularly write to in English. Does she/he work in your company or for another company? How do you begin your email? How do you end it? Use the phrases from the page opposite to help you complete the email below.

To: ....
Subject: ....

Greeting: ....
Opening sentence: ....

Closing sentence: ....
Close: ....

11 Think of two more people you often write to. Write the beginning and ending of the emails you would send them. Are they all the same or different? Compare your emails with a partner.

Last but not least

12 This question was discussed on an online forum: "Do I really need to use a greeting and a close in all my emails?" Read the comments and discuss with a partner. What do *you* think?

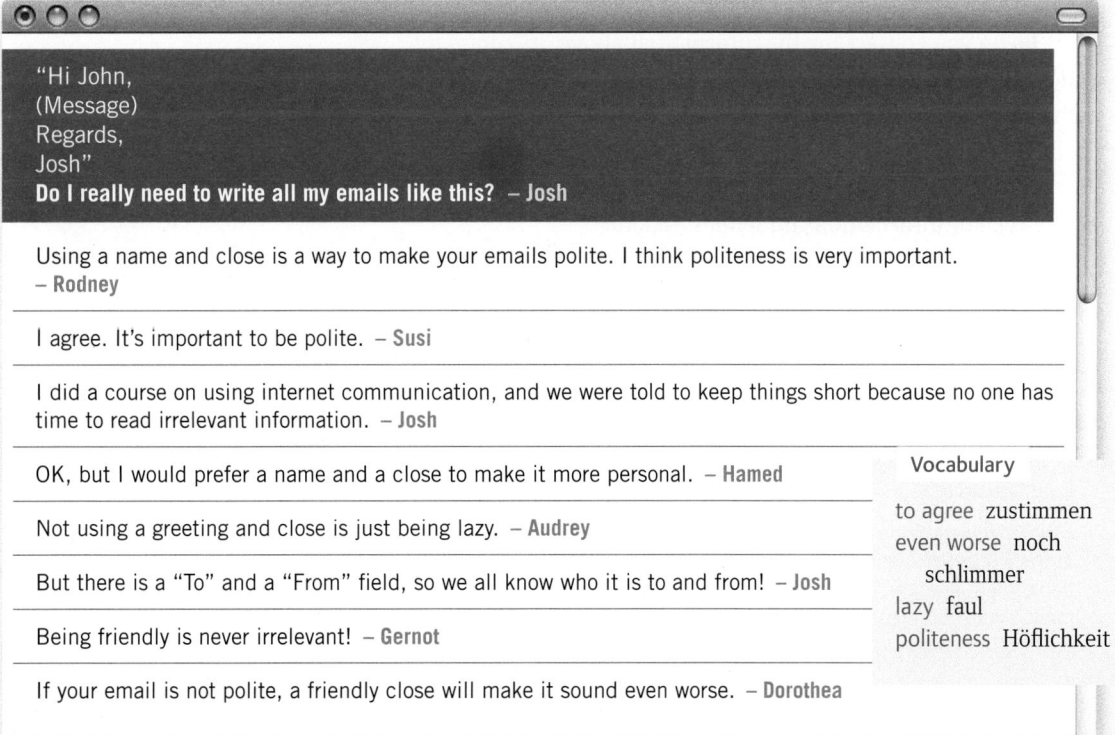

"Hi John,
(Message)
Regards,
Josh"
Do I really need to write all my emails like this? – Josh

Using a name and close is a way to make your emails polite. I think politeness is very important. – Rodney

I agree. It's important to be polite. – Susi

I did a course on using internet communication, and we were told to keep things short because no one has time to read irrelevant information. – Josh

OK, but I would prefer a name and a close to make it more personal. – Hamed

Not using a greeting and close is just being lazy. – Audrey

But there is a "To" and a "From" field, so we all know who it is to and from! – Josh

Being friendly is never irrelevant! – Gernot

If your email is not polite, a friendly close will make it sound even worse. – Dorothea

Vocabulary

to agree zustimmen
even worse noch
   schlimmer
lazy faul
politeness Höflichkeit

Learning objectives

- Asking colleagues for information
  Kollegen und Kolleginnen um Informationen bitten
- Writing inquiries to new contacts
  Neuen Kontakten Anfragen schicken

2 Asking for Information

1 What type of information do you sometimes ask for in emails?
Tick the correct boxes on the left.

	in-company colleagues	external contacts
information about products or prices	☐	☐
a quote for products or services	☐	☐
details of times and dates (for a meeting, etc.)	☐	☐
contact information (names, addresses, phone numbers)	☐	☐
technical information	☐	☐
information about rules and regulations	☐	☐
other	☐	☐

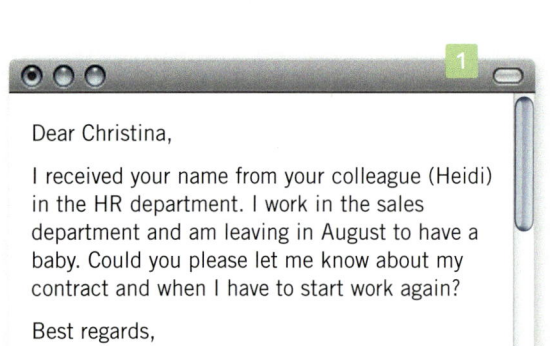

Who do you contact for the information above: in-company colleagues or external contacts? Tick the correct boxes on the right and compare your answers with a partner.

Vocabulary

quote/quotation Angebot
rules and regulations Vorschriften
services Dienstleistungen

2 Read the four emails below and opposite, and match them to the type of information the sender asks for.

a ☐ contact information
b ☐ times or dates
c ☐ rules and regulations
d ☐ personal information

! personal = persönlich
personnel = das Personal

1

Dear Christina,

I received your name from your colleague (Heidi) in the HR department. I work in the sales department and am leaving in August to have a baby. Could you please let me know about my contract and when I have to start work again?

Best regards,
Petra

2

Dear Georg,

I'd like some information about the new client. We're visiting him next week so I need a copy of the "customer profile". Can you please send it as an attachment to me?

Thank you,
Stacy

some information
(not ~~an information~~)
(not ~~informations~~)

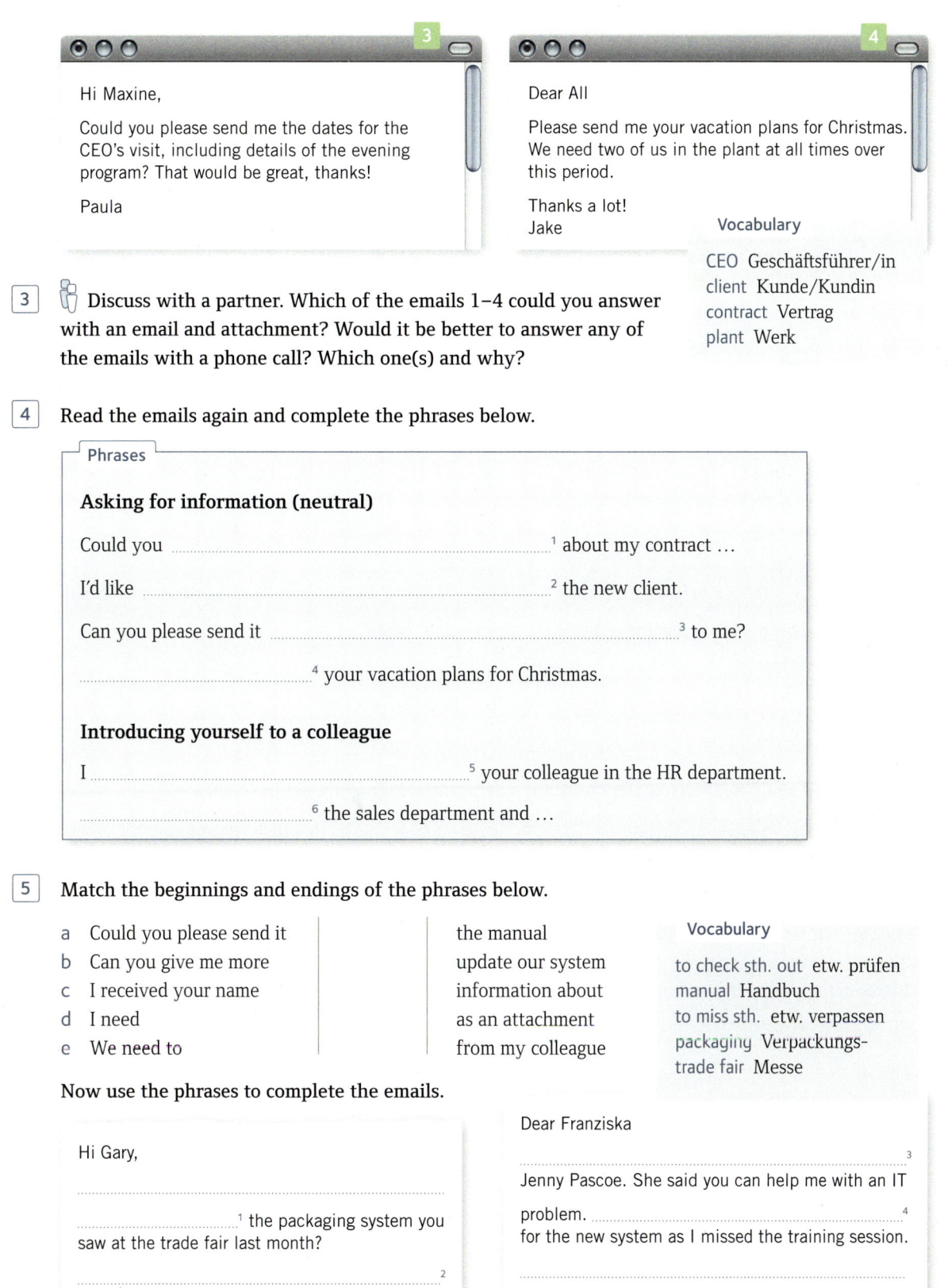

3

Hi Maxine,

Could you please send me the dates for the CEO's visit, including details of the evening program? That would be great, thanks!

Paula

4

Dear All

Please send me your vacation plans for Christmas. We need two of us in the plant at all times over this period.

Thanks a lot!
Jake

Vocabulary

CEO Geschäftsführer/in
client Kunde/Kundin
contract Vertrag
plant Werk

3 Discuss with a partner. Which of the emails 1–4 could you answer with an email and attachment? Would it be better to answer any of the emails with a phone call? Which one(s) and why?

4 Read the emails again and complete the phrases below.

> **Phrases**
>
> **Asking for information (neutral)**
>
> Could you ....¹ about my contract …
>
> I'd like ....² the new client.
>
> Can you please send it ....³ to me?
>
> ....⁴ your vacation plans for Christmas.
>
> **Introducing yourself to a colleague**
>
> I ....⁵ your colleague in the HR department.
>
> ....⁶ the sales department and …

5 Match the beginnings and endings of the phrases below.

a Could you please send it   the manual

b Can you give me more   update our system

c I received your name   information about

d I need   as an attachment

e We need to   from my colleague

Vocabulary

to check sth. out etw. prüfen
manual Handbuch
to miss sth. etw. verpassen
packaging Verpackungs-
trade fair Messe

Now use the phrases to complete the emails.

Hi Gary,

....

....¹ the packaging system you saw at the trade fair last month?

....²

so I'm checking out what's on the market.

Thanks,
Martin

Dear Franziska

....³

Jenny Pascoe. She said you can help me with an IT

problem. ....⁴
for the new system as I missed the training session.

....

....⁵ to me?

Thank you.
Jamie

6 ◁ 04 Martin doesn't receive an answer to his email (in exercise 5) so he calls Gary to get the contact information. Listen to the phone call and take notes. What does Gary ask Martin to do?

Now use your notes to fill in the gaps below.

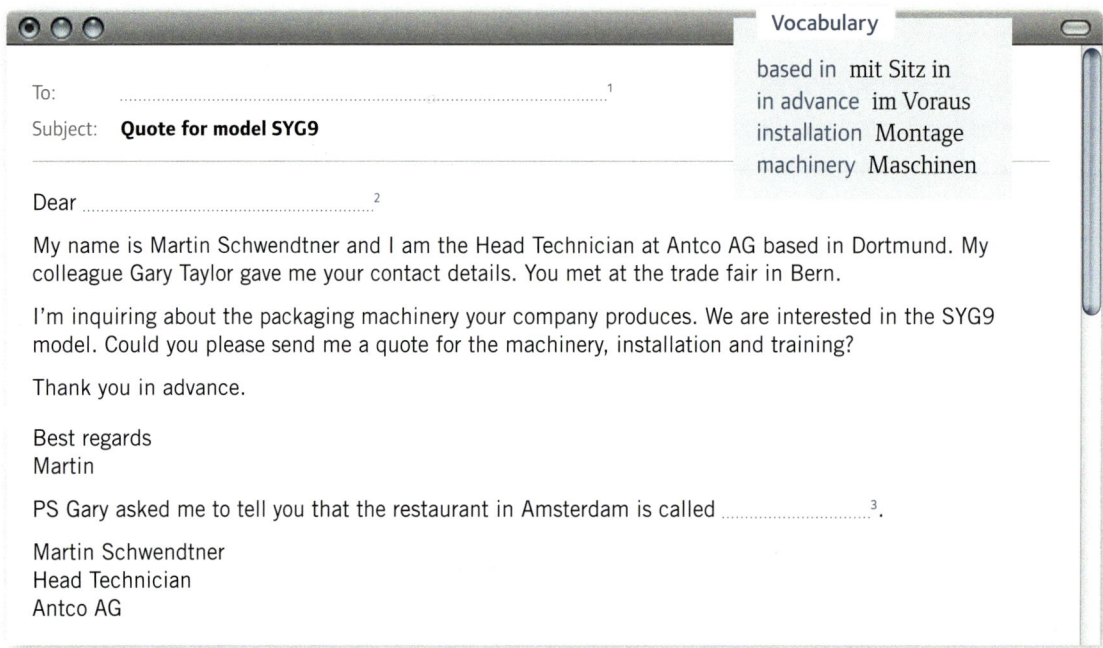

To: ....¹

Subject: **Quote for model SYG9**

Vocabulary
based in mit Sitz in
in advance im Voraus
installation Montage
machinery Maschinen

Dear ....²

My name is Martin Schwendtner and I am the Head Technician at Antco AG based in Dortmund. My colleague Gary Taylor gave me your contact details. You met at the trade fair in Bern.

I'm inquiring about the packaging machinery your company produces. We are interested in the SYG9 model. Could you please send me a quote for the machinery, installation and training?

Thank you in advance.

Best regards
Martin

PS Gary asked me to tell you that the restaurant in Amsterdam is called ....³.

Martin Schwendtner
Head Technician
Antco AG

7 Read the email again and answer the questions, then complete the phrases in the box.

1 How does Martin begin his email?
  ▢ with information about himself
  ▢ by asking for information

2 What type of information does Martin want?
  ▢ a price
  ▢ a brochure

Phrases

Introducing yourself to a business partner

My name is …

I ....¹ Head Technician at Antco AG ....² Dortmund.

My colleague gave ....³.

Asking for information (more formal)

I am writing to request some information about …

I am contacting you because …

I'm ....⁴ the packaging machinery your company produces.

We ....⁵ the SYG9 model.
---

8 Which words and phrases below can you use with a new contact? Match words and phrases that mean the same and sort them into the table.

Can you let us know …?

to buy

to ask about sth.

Could you please tell us …?

Thank you

to inquire about sth.

We need to get …

to ask for sth.

to request sth.

to purchase

We are interested in getting …

Thanks

more formal (for first contacts)	neutral (for colleagues)
Thank you	Thanks

9 Choose the correct phrases to complete this email to a new contact.

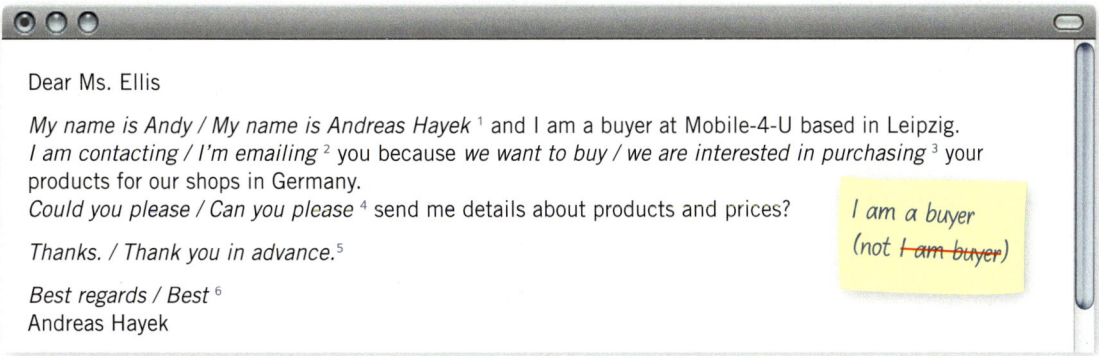

Dear Ms. Ellis

My name is Andy / My name is Andreas Hayek [1] and I am a buyer at Mobile-4-U based in Leipzig.
I am contacting / I'm emailing [2] you because *we want to buy / we are interested in purchasing* [3] your products for our shops in Germany.
Could you please / Can you please [4] send me details about products and prices?

Thanks. / Thank you in advance. [5]

Best regards / Best [6]
Andreas Hayek

*I am a buyer
(not ~~I am buyer~~)*

10 Translate the sentences below into English to write an email to a new contact.

1 Liebe Frau Armstrong
2 Ich bin Technikerin bei der Media Systems.
3 Ihren Namen habe ich von Ihrer Kollegin im Berliner Büro.
4 Ich kontaktiere Sie, da wir an Ihren Qualitätstests *(quality tests)* interessiert sind.
5 Könnten Sie uns die Ergebnisse *(results)* bitte im Anhang schicken?
6 Vielen Dank im Voraus.
7 Mit freundlichen Grüßen

Key phrases

Here are some key phrases from the unit. Tick the ones that are useful for you.

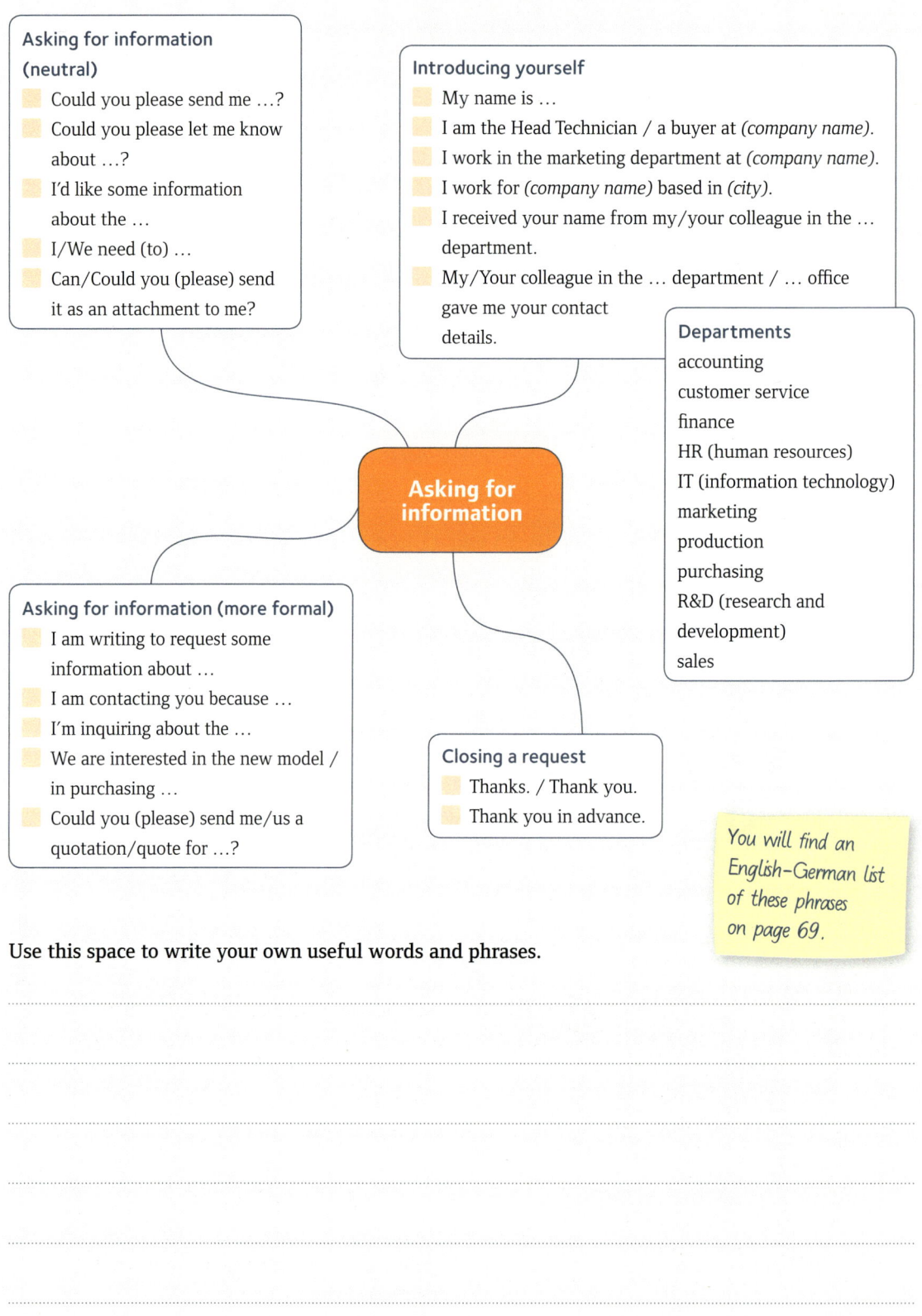

Asking for information (neutral)
- ☐ Could you please send me …?
- ☐ Could you please let me know about …?
- ☐ I'd like some information about the …
- ☐ I/We need (to) …
- ☐ Can/Could you (please) send it as an attachment to me?

Introducing yourself
- ☐ My name is …
- ☐ I am the Head Technician / a buyer at (company name).
- ☐ I work in the marketing department at (company name).
- ☐ I work for (company name) based in (city).
- ☐ I received your name from my/your colleague in the … department.
- ☐ My/Your colleague in the … department / … office gave me your contact details.

Departments
accounting
customer service
finance
HR (human resources)
IT (information technology)
marketing
production
purchasing
R&D (research and development)
sales

Asking for information

Asking for information (more formal)
- ☐ I am writing to request some information about …
- ☐ I am contacting you because …
- ☐ I'm inquiring about the …
- ☐ We are interested in the new model / in purchasing …
- ☐ Could you (please) send me/us a quotation/quote for …?

Closing a request
- ☐ Thanks. / Thank you.
- ☐ Thank you in advance.

You will find an English-German list of these phrases on page 69.

Use this space to write your own useful words and phrases.

....

....

....

....

....

....

Over to you

11 You want to write two emails – one to someone you know and one to a new contact. First fill in the information below, then write one of the emails.

Someone you know

Name:

....

Information you need:

....

....

Why you need the information:

....

....

....

New contact

Name:

....

How you got his/her name:

....

Information about YOU:

– Job: ....

– Company: ....

Information you need + why:

....

....

 Swap emails with a partner. Can you tell whether your partner's email is to a new contact or to a colleague? How? Now write your second email and compare the phrases you use.

Last but not least

12  In pairs, read the article below from a business blog. Which tips do you think are the most useful? Why do you and your partner read (or not read) the emails you receive?

Vocabulary

to avoid vermeiden
to be busy viel zu tun haben
busy times Stoßzeiten
to make sure versichern
tone Tonfall

Making sure your email is read

Tone
Try to connect with the person you're writing to. With new contacts, write to a specific person (not "Sir or Madam") and use the right tone – not too informal and not too formal.

Message
Your message should be simple, short and easy to read. Make sure it's clear to the reader what you want and what the reader should do. Make it easy for them to answer your question, send you product details, or call you.

Subject line
Statistics say that people only open 20–40% of the emails they receive, but they read all of the subject lines. This shows how important subject lines are, so make sure they are short, attractive and, if possible, personal.

Timing
Contact your colleague or client when they are not too busy. The best times to send emails are in the middle of the week and at midday. Avoid busy times like Monday mornings.

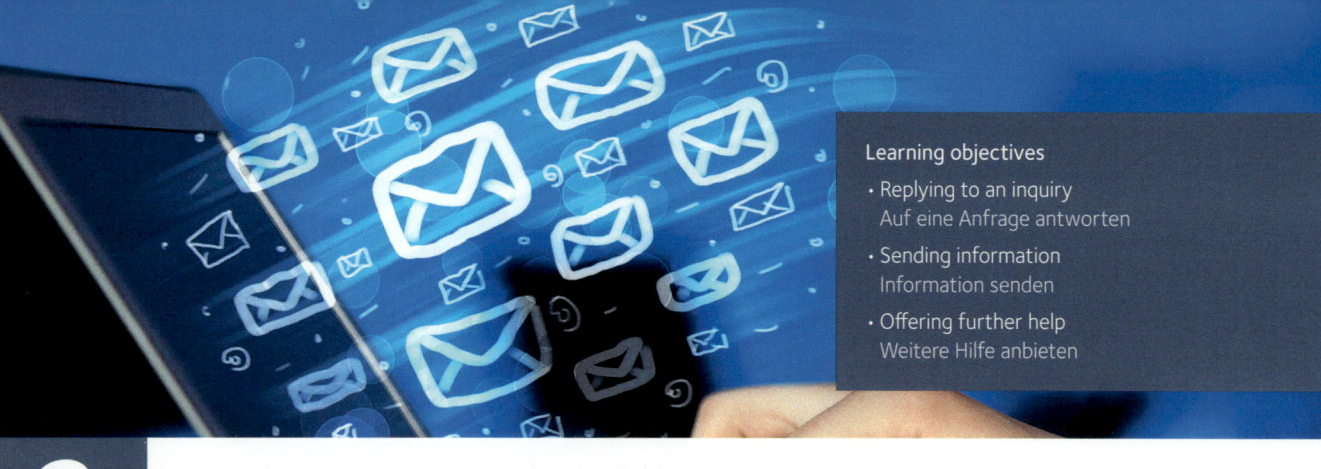

Learning objectives
- Replying to an inquiry
  Auf eine Anfrage antworten
- Sending information
  Information senden
- Offering further help
  Weitere Hilfe anbieten

3 Giving information

1 What type of information do you send people in emails? Tick the correct boxes and compare your answers with a partner.

information …
- ☐ about products or services
- ☐ about contacts (e. g. phone numbers and email addresses)
- ☐ needed to make appointments
- ☐ concerning daily operations
- ☐ other ....

....

or …
- ☐ reports
- ☐ results
- ☐ updates

> **Vocabulary**
>
> appointment Termin
> daily operations Tagesgeschäft
> report Bericht
> results Ergebnisse

2 Read the subject lines below and match them to the emails 1–4.

a ☐ Subject: Re: Vacation info needed
b ☐ Subject: Re: Your experience with the new machinery
c ☐ Subject: Re: Inquiry – FORTUN product line
d ☐ Subject: Re: Packaging system request

1

Dear Mr. Suppinger

Thank you for your interest in our products. Please find our PDF brochure in the attachment. It contains all the product specifications and the price list.

Please contact me if you have further questions. We would be happy to arrange a meeting to discuss your requirements.

Regards
Nigel Johnston

2

To: Marcia
From: Anke

Regarding the vacation dates you need, I've attached a spreadsheet with the details for your team.

See you at the meeting next week.

A

> **Vocabulary**
>
> experience Erfahrung
> inquiry Anfrage
> request Anfrage, Bitte
> requirements Anforderungen
> spreadsheet Tabelle

3

Hello Conny,

Thanks for your email – it's nice to hear from you again.

We have had the new machinery for six months and find it very good. There were some problems at the beginning, but now the system is performing exactly as we hoped.

Please find our summary attached.

Let me know if you have any more questions. I'd be glad to give you a demonstration if you can come to our Toulouse plant.

Best wishes,
Philippe

4

Dear Michael,

Thank you for contacting me. I remember Laura from the trade fair.

We have a wide range of packaging systems – Laura was interested in the ActionX line.

You can use the link below to find a full description of all of our systems.

KPT packaging systems

Feel free to contact me if you need anything else.

Best regards,
Sergei

Vocabulary

a wide range of eine breite Palette an
to perform funktionieren
summary Zusammenfassung

Discuss with a partner. Which emails are replying to …

a   a colleague or someone the writer knows? ....

b   a first-time contact? ....

How do you know?

3   Read the emails again and complete the phrases below.

Phrases

Beginning a reply

Thank you for .... [1] our products.

.... [2] the vacation dates you need, …

.... [3] email – it's nice to hear from you again.

Sending information

Please find our PDF .... [4],

… I've .... [5] a spreadsheet with …

You can use .... [6] to find a full description of …

Offering further help

Please contact me if you .... [7].

.... [8] you have any more questions.

I'd be .... [9] a demonstration …

Feel free .... [10] if you need anything else.

---

4 Match the sentences halves in each group. Connect them with a line, as in the example.

1 I am attaching   the link below to download the brochure.
  You can use   the price list you wanted.
  Please find   the information attached.

2 We would be   glad to send you more information.
  Feel free to   contact me if you have further questions.

3 Thank you for your   contacting me.
  Thank you for   interest.

Where would you find each group of sentences (1–3) in an email?

a ▨ at the beginning   b ▨ in the middle   c ▨ at the end

5 Decide which is the more formal of each pair.

1 a ▨ Thank you, I received the report yesterday.
  b ▨ Thank you, I got the report yesterday.

2 a ▨ Looking forward to your answer.
  b ▨ I look forward to your reply.

3 a ▨ I attended a meeting last week.
  b ▨ I went to a meeting last week.

4 a ▨ We'd like to help you with your problem.
  b ▨ We would like to assist you with your problem.

5 a ▨ Please inform me of any changes.
  b ▨ Please let me know if anything has changed.

6 👥 Read the two emails below and discuss with a partner: What do Mr. Schöberl and Sandra need to send and how formal should their replies be?

Vocabulary

to assist   helfen
to attend   besuchen
quality assurance   Qualitätssicherung
questionnaire   Fragebogen
research   Forschung

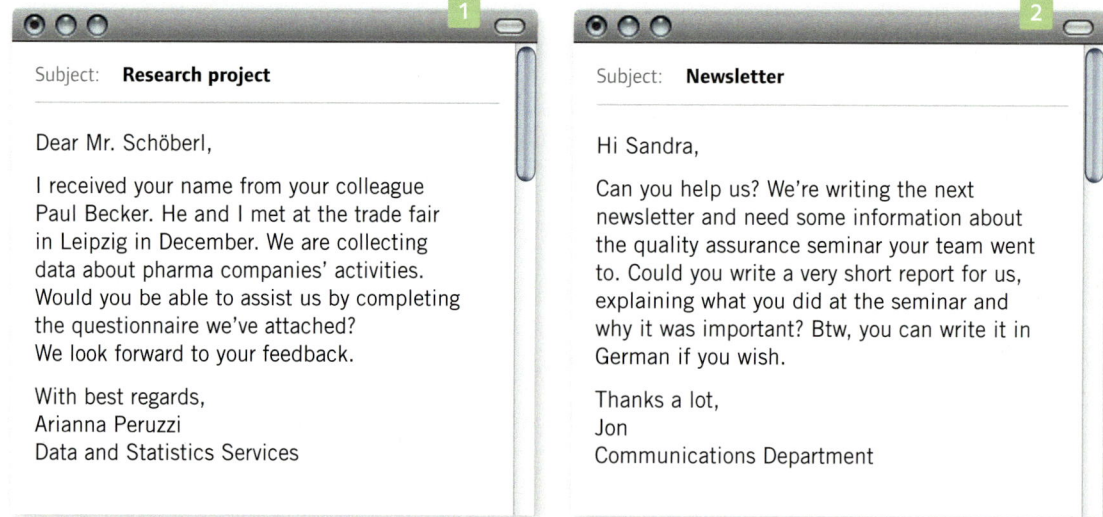

1

Subject: **Research project**

Dear Mr. Schöberl,

I received your name from your colleague Paul Becker. He and I met at the trade fair in Leipzig in December. We are collecting data about pharma companies' activities. Would you be able to assist us by completing the questionnaire we've attached? We look forward to your feedback.

With best regards,
Arianna Peruzzi
Data and Statistics Services

2

Subject: **Newsletter**

Hi Sandra,

Can you help us? We're writing the next newsletter and need some information about the quality assurance seminar your team went to. Could you write a very short report for us, explaining what you did at the seminar and why it was important? Btw, you can write it in German if you wish.

Thanks a lot,
Jon
Communications Department

7 Put the sentences in the correct order to write the replies.

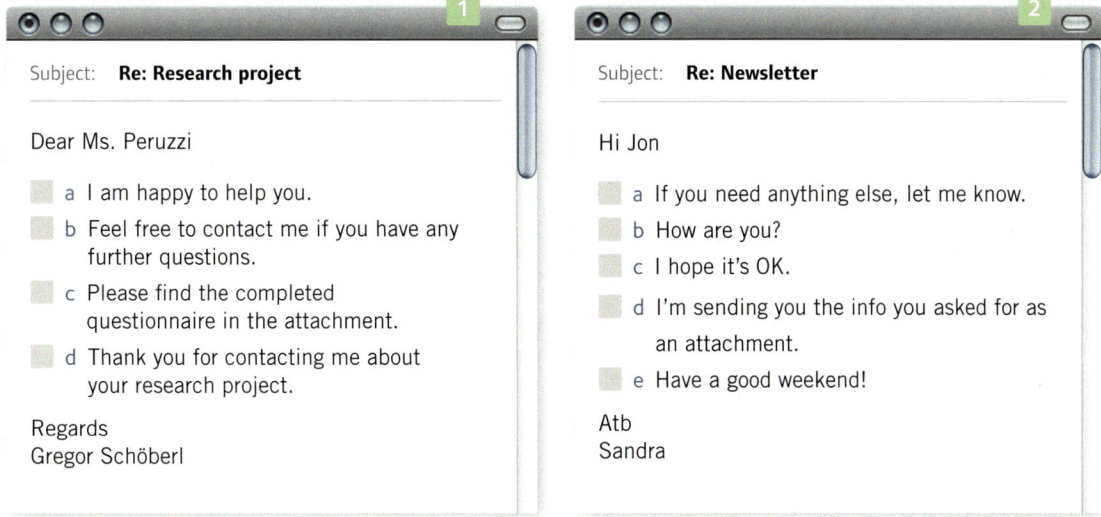

1

Subject: **Re: Research project**

Dear Ms. Peruzzi

☐ a I am happy to help you.

☐ b Feel free to contact me if you have any further questions.

☐ c Please find the completed questionnaire in the attachment.

☐ d Thank you for contacting me about your research project.

Regards
Gregor Schöberl

2

Subject: **Re: Newsletter**

Hi Jon

☐ a If you need anything else, let me know.

☐ b How are you?

☐ c I hope it's OK.

☐ d I'm sending you the info you asked for as an attachment.

☐ e Have a good weekend!

Atb
Sandra

Did you know?

When writing informal emails, especially ones to friends or close colleagues, some people use abbreviations or short forms such as "btw", "atb" or "info". Even if you don't use them, it's helpful to know what they mean.

8 Match these abbreviations or short forms with their meaning.

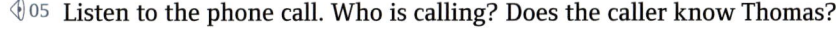

atb · btw · dept. · e.g. · etc. · fyi · info · re

1 for example ....

2 information ....

3 for your information ....

4 et cetera ....

5 regarding ....

6 department ....

7 all the best ....

8 by the way ....

9 ◁05 Listen to the phone call. Who is calling? Does the caller know Thomas?

Listen again. What does the caller want from Thomas? Tick the correct boxes.

the test results on the
☐ 50 ml bottles
☐ 100 ml bottles
☐ 150 ml bottles

a copy of the
☐ meeting planner
☐ shift planner
☐ vacation planner

Vocabulary

planner Planer
to refer to sth. auf
    etw. Bezug nehmen
shift Schicht

10 Now write Thomas' email. Decide how formal the email should be and follow the steps below. You can start like this if you wish:
It was nice speaking to you this morning.

· Refer to the phone call.
· Give the information (in an attachment and/or a link)
· Offer further help

Here are some key phrases from the unit. Tick the ones that are useful for you.

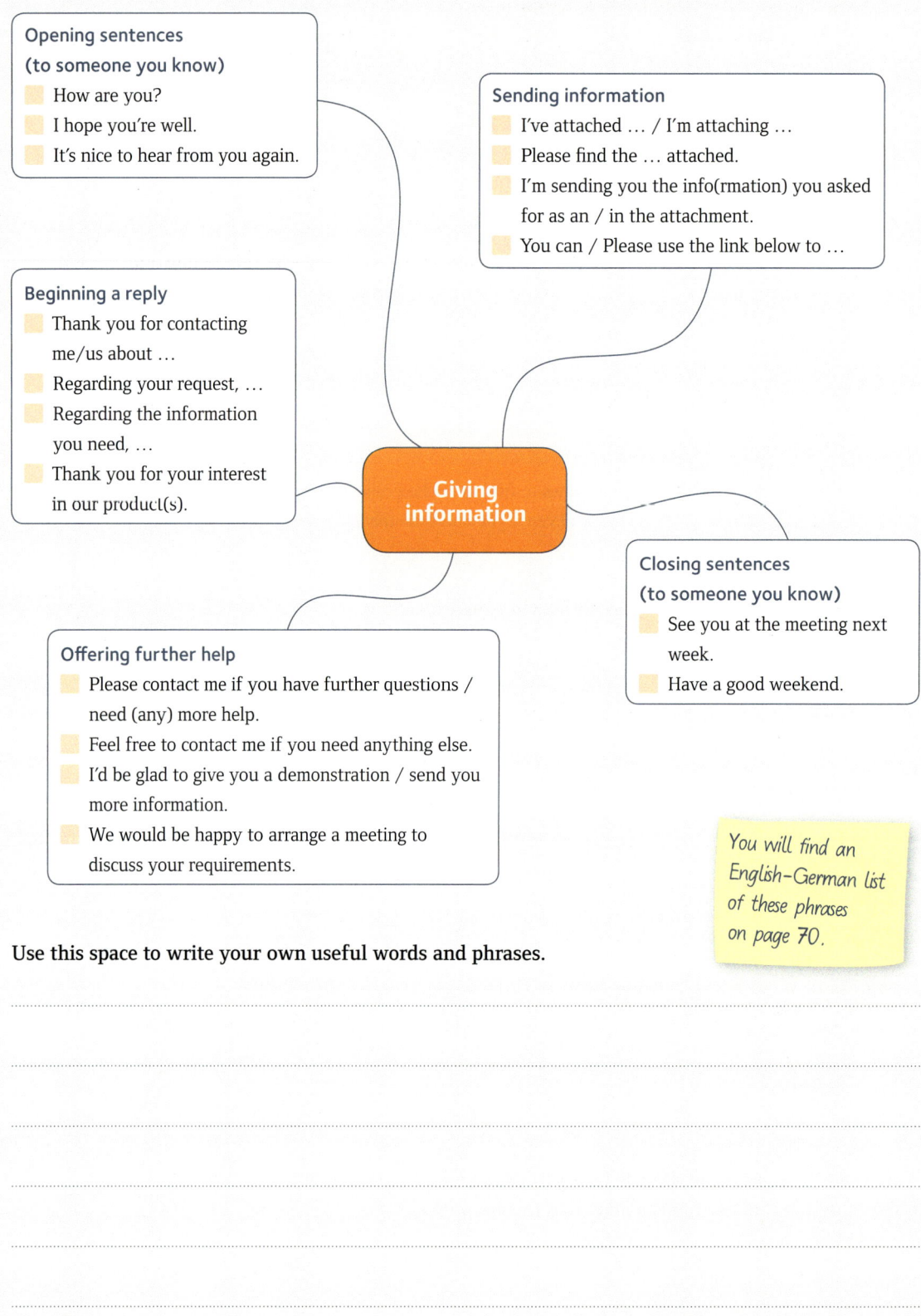

**Opening sentences
(to someone you know)**
- How are you?
- I hope you're well.
- It's nice to hear from you again.

Sending information
- I've attached … / I'm attaching …
- Please find the … attached.
- I'm sending you the info(rmation) you asked for as an / in the attachment.
- You can / Please use the link below to …

Beginning a reply
- Thank you for contacting me/us about …
- Regarding your request, …
- Regarding the information you need, …
- Thank you for your interest in our product(s).

Giving information

**Closing sentences
(to someone you know)**
- See you at the meeting next week.
- Have a good weekend.

Offering further help
- Please contact me if you have further questions / need (any) more help.
- Feel free to contact me if you need anything else.
- I'd be glad to give you a demonstration / send you more information.
- We would be happy to arrange a meeting to discuss your requirements.

You will find an English–German list of these phrases on page 70.

Use this space to write your own useful words and phrases.

....

....

....

....

....

....

Over to you

11 Think of an inquiry you received recently. Who was it from? What information did the person need? Use the key phrases opposite to write a reply.

Swap emails with a partner. How did your partner send the information? (info in the email? attachment? link? text message? phone call later?) Is your partner's email to a person they know well or to a new contact?

Last but not least

12 What are the different ways of sending information? Look at the diagram below and, with a partner, add a–e to the gaps 1–5. Can you add any more ways of sending information (line 6)?

a   give link (using cloud services or the intranet)
b   forward email to correct person
c   send calendar invitation (using software)
d   send PDF as attachment
e   send digital business card as text message

Vocabulary

instant message (im) Sofortnachricht
invitation Einladung
text (message) SMS

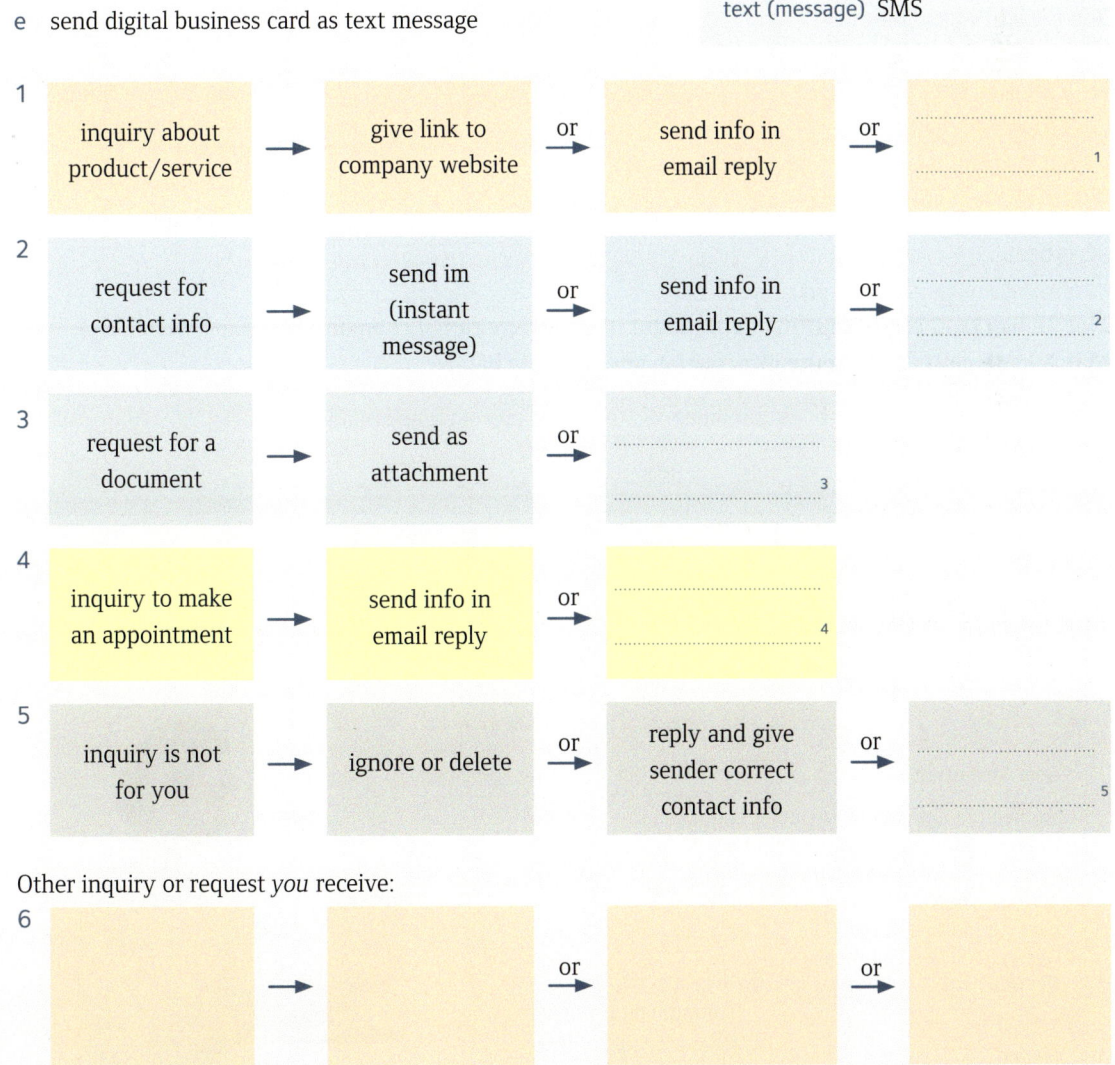

1

| inquiry about product/service | → | give link to company website | or → | send info in email reply | or → | .... 1 |

2

| request for contact info | → | send im (instant message) | or → | send info in email reply | or → | .... 2 |

3

| request for a document | → | send as attachment | or → | .... 3 |

4

| inquiry to make an appointment | → | send info in email reply | or → | .... 4 |

5

| inquiry is not for you | → | ignore or delete | or → | reply and give sender correct contact info | or → | .... 5 |

Other inquiry or request *you* receive:

6

| | → | | or → | | or → | |

Learning objectives
- Following up unanswered emails
  Unbeantwortete E-Mails weiterverfolgen
- Sending reminders
  Erinnerungen schicken
- Giving a deadline
  Eine Frist setzen

4 Requesting action

1 Sometimes people don't send you the information you asked for. Tick the situations that are relevant for you, then compare your list with a partner.

You are still waiting for …

- [ ] an answer to an email
- [ ] a decision
- [ ] a payment
- [ ] a document, e.g. a report, minutes, a contract
- [ ] discussion points for an agenda

- [ ] other ....

Vocabulary

agenda Tagesordnung
decision Entscheidung
payment Zahlung

2 Marion works in the accounting department of an international company based in Switzerland. Match her emails (1–3) to the information she requests below.

a ☐ agenda points b ☐ payment c ☐ customer information

1

Dear Marcel

This is a gentle reminder. Please see email below sent two weeks ago. Thanks for your support.

Best
M

> Dear Marcel
>
> We need to update our customer contacts in the new software. Please check the list attached and update anything that isn't correct. I need the list back by the end of the week so that we can meet the deadline.
>
> Thanks
> Marion

2

Hi Sofia

The team meeting is next week, so could you please send me your points for the agenda asap? I need them by Friday at the latest.

Thanks!
Marion

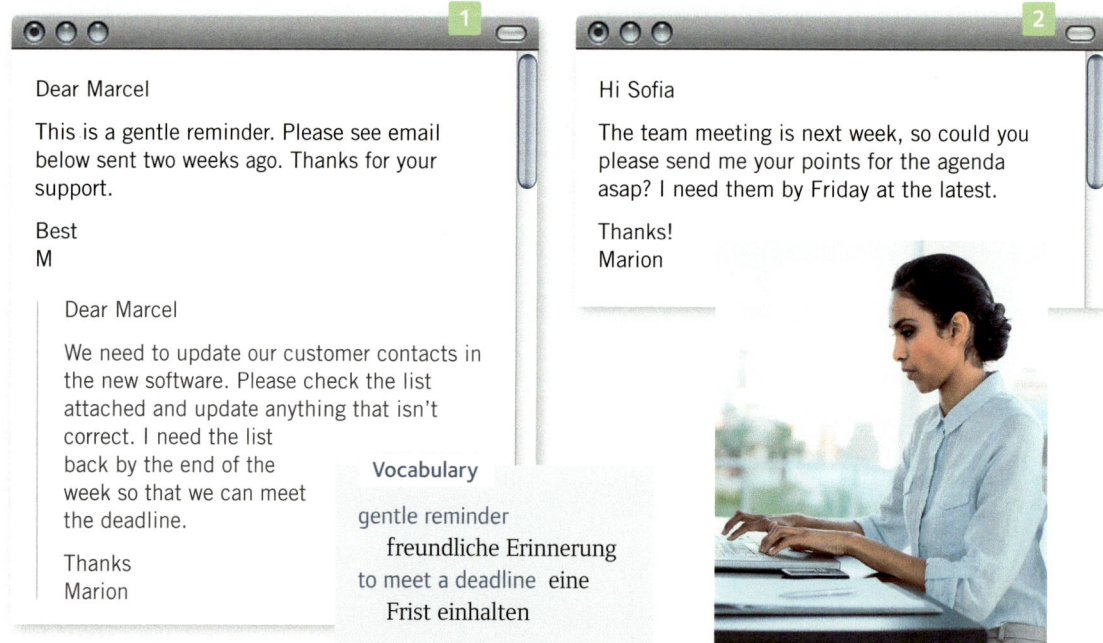

Vocabulary

gentle reminder
  freundliche Erinnerung
to meet a deadline eine
  Frist einhalten

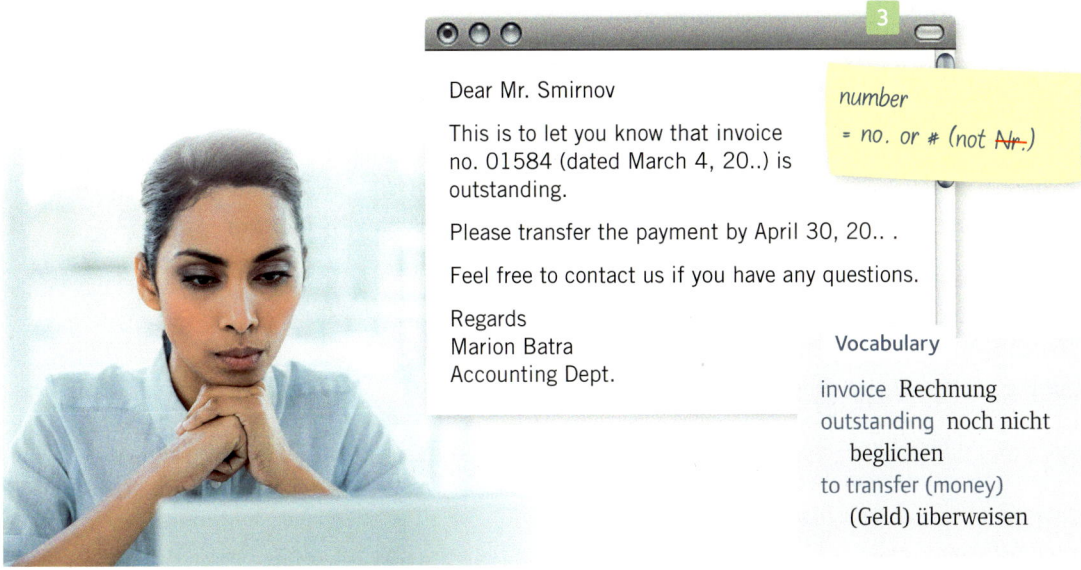

Dear Mr. Smirnov

This is to let you know that invoice no. 01584 (dated March 4, 20..) is outstanding.

Please transfer the payment by April 30, 20.. .

Feel free to contact us if you have any questions.

Regards
Marion Batra
Accounting Dept.

number
= no. or # (not Nr.)

Vocabulary

invoice Rechnung
outstanding noch nicht
   beglichen
to transfer (money)
   (Geld) überweisen

Did you know?

You can use the following structure when requesting action.

Explain the situation: Make sure your contact knows why you are writing before you make your request.

Request action: Say exactly what you need.

Give a deadline: Say when you need it.

Use a friendly close: Thank the contact for his/her support or offer further help.

---

3 Read the emails again and complete the phrases below.

Phrases

Explaining the situation

This is ....¹ reminder.

I am writing concerning the contract.

We ....² our customer contacts.

This is ....³ invoice no. … is outstanding.

Requesting action

Please ....⁴ and update anything that isn't correct.

… could you please ....⁵ for the agenda asap?

Please ....⁶ by April 30, 20.. .

Giving a deadline

I need the list back ....⁷ the week so we can meet the deadline.

I need them ....⁸ .

4 Match the parts of the sentences.

1 This is to let you know that   a the payment.
2 Could you please update me   b reminder.
3 Please contact me about   c the contract is ready.
4 This is a gentle   d that the invoice is still outstanding.
5 I am writing to let you know   e on the project?

Which of the sentences above are:

opening sentences? ....   requests? ....

5 Read the sentences and choose the best time word or phrase.

1 The report needs to be on my desk *on Friday / two days ago.*
2 Please send me the update *by / on* next week.
3 We sent the invoice *a month ago / by Tuesday* and it is still
   outstanding.
4 Please transfer the payment *by / on* the end of the week.
5 We need all your comments *by Wednesday / a week ago* so that
   we can present them at the meeting *by / on* Friday.
6 We asked you for the information *by Monday / five days ago.*
   Can you please reply asap?

I need the report by Thursday.
(not until Thursday)
= bis Donnerstag

The meeting is on Monday.
= am Montag

I sent an email two days ago.
= vor zwei Tagen

Now make some sentences about requests and deadlines
that are true for you and tell a partner.

I/We … ago.

Could you please … by …?

We need … by …
so that we can … on …

6 Complete the emails below and opposite with the following phrases.

a get back to me asap, please
b Could you please send
c I spoke to your colleague
d by tomorrow morning
e a few days ago
f as soon as possible

Vocabulary

to get back to antworten
to place an order eine
   Bestellung aufgeben
to process bearbeiten

○ ○ ○

Subject: **Your order #289H3 – answers needed**

Hello Paolo,

I'm contacting you about the order you placed last week.

I sent you a list of questions ....[1] – see email below. Can you answer them and

............................[2]? I need the answers ....

............................[3] at the latest so that I can process your order this week.

Thanks,
Ulrike

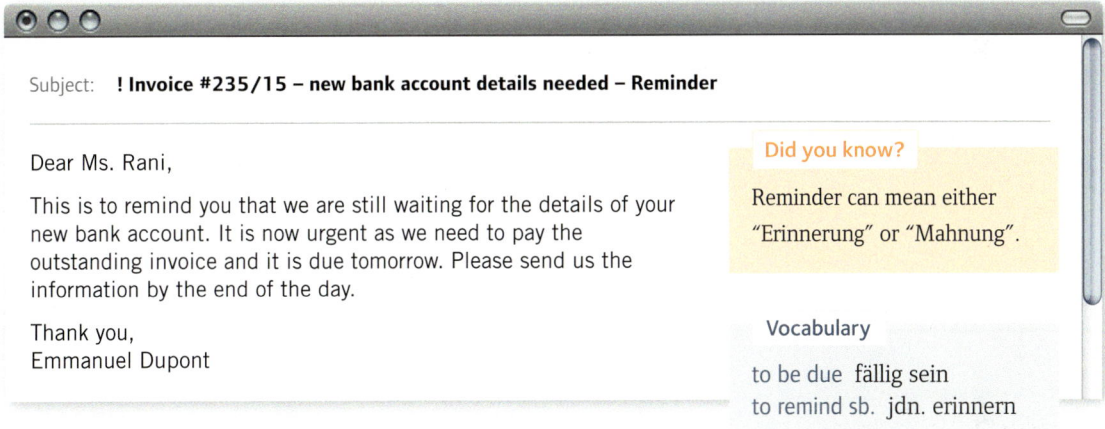

Subject: **Invoice #235/15 – new bank account details needed**

> not yet
> = noch nicht

Dear Ms. Rani,

.... [4] about your company's new bank account details two days ago.
We agreed she would send me an email with the information, but unfortunately I have not received it yet.
.... [5] the account details to me .... [6]
so we can pay the above invoice on time?

Thank you in advance.
Regards,
Emmanuel Dupont

Vocabulary

bank account Bankkonto
on time pünktlich
unfortunately leider

---

7 Emmanuel does not receive a reply from Ms. Rani so he sends a follow-up message. Read the email below. How is this email different from the one above? Discuss with a partner.

Subject: **! Invoice #235/15 – new bank account details needed – Reminder**

Dear Ms. Rani,

This is to remind you that we are still waiting for the details of your new bank account. It is now urgent as we need to pay the outstanding invoice and it is due tomorrow. Please send us the information by the end of the day.

Thank you,
Emmanuel Dupont

Did you know?

Reminder can mean either "Erinnerung" or "Mahnung".

Vocabulary

to be due fällig sein
to remind sb. jdn. erinnern

---

8 The following sentences are useful for saying that something is urgent. Match the sentence halves.

1 Please get back to me as soon as	a as we have to send in the report today.
2 It is important that we receive	b possible so we can process your order.
3 Unfortunately, it is now urgent	c it right away? We need it this week.
4 Can you please send	d your decision by the end of the day.

---

9 🔊 06 Bob Haslam and Karina Meyer are discussing an outstanding invoice from one of their customers, Baxwell Ltd. in the UK. Listen and tick the correct boxes.

1 The customer wants to place a ___ small ⬜ large ⬜ order.
2 The invoice number is ___ 201614 ⬜ 201640 ⬜.
3 The payment was due ___ two ⬜ three ⬜ weeks ago.
4 Karina should tell John Leach that the payment is ___ urgent ⬜ due today ⬜.
5 John needs to ___ call back ⬜ pay the invoice ⬜ before they can start on the order.
6 John should contact ___ Karina ⬜ Bob ⬜ Karina or Bob ⬜ if he has any questions.

Work with a partner and write Karina's email to John Leach. You can start the email like this if you wish: *I am writing about the order you would like to place. Unfortunately, …*

Here are some key phrases from the unit. Tick the ones that are useful for you.

Explaining the situation

- This is to let you know that invoice no. … is outstanding.
- I am writing to let you know that …
- I am writing about/concerning/ regarding …
- This is a gentle reminder.
- I spoke to your colleague … two days ago.

Giving a deadline

- Please get back to me by April 30.
- I need the information by Friday at the latest.
- I need the list back by the end of the week.
- The list needs to be on my desk by/on Thursday.
- The payment/report is due tomorrow.

Requesting action

- Please transfer the payment / check the list / send me …
- Could you please send …?

Requesting action

Saying something is urgent

- Please get back to me / contact me as soon as possible so that we can …
- Please reply/answer as soon as you can.
- It is important that we receive your decision / the report by the end of the day/week.
- Unfortunately, … is now urgent as we need to …
- Could/Can you please send it right away?

You will find an English–German list of these phrases on page 71.

Use this space to write your own useful words and phrases.

....

....

....

....

....

....

Over to you

10 Look back at exercise 1 on page 24. Choose a situation where you need to request action, and complete the card.

What you need: ....

Who you need it from: .... (colleague, business partner, etc.)

When you need it: ....

Now write the email, using the steps below and the key phrases opposite to help you structure your email. Don't forget to write a clear subject line.

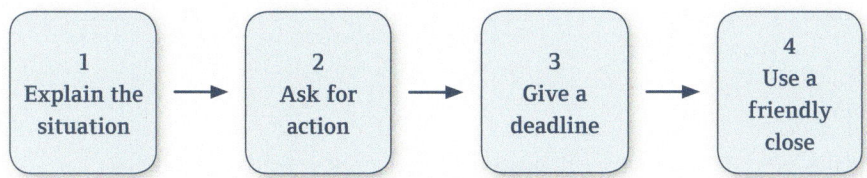

1 Explain the situation → **2** Ask for action → **3** Give a deadline → **4** Use a friendly close

Swap emails with a partner. Is your partner's email polite? Is it clear what the reader needs to do and by when?

11 It is a week (or more) later and you are still waiting for the information that you requested … and now it is urgent! Write a second email, then compare emails with a partner.

Last but not least

12 Read this tip from a business blog.

> "What is important is seldom urgent and what is urgent is seldom important."
> *Dwight D. Eisenhower*

www.emailing-tips.com

URGENT

Tip #4: the high priority button

Try not to add the "high priority" or "urgent" symbol to your emails too often. If you use it too much, your colleagues or business partners will get used to seeing it and might ignore your emails that really *are* important. If the email is *really* urgent, and you decide that you need to use the symbol, make sure the message is urgent for *both* you *and* the person you are writing to. In general, though, instead of using the button, it is more effective to have a clear subject line that shows the recipient right away that the email needs a quick answer.

Discuss the questions below with a partner.

1 Do you use the urgent (!) symbol for your emails? Which emails do you use it for?

2 How do you feel when you get an email with the urgent symbol? Do you agree with the tip?

Vocabulary

to get used to doing sth. sich daran gewöhnen, etw. zu tun
to ignore nicht beachten
recipient Empfänger/in
seldom selten

Giving updates

Learning objectives

• Asking for and giving an update
  Ein Update einfordern und geben

• Giving reasons
  Gründe angeben

• Making suggestions
  Vorschläge machen

---

1 Discuss with a partner.

1 Who do you send updates to?
2 Who sends you updates?

3 Are updates a regular activity in your job, or do you just give and get them when you are working on a project?

2 Read the two emails below. Who is asking for the update and why? Does he get the information he needs?

Vocabulary

to hear back from sb. eine Antwort
  von jdm. bekommen
pricing Preisgestaltung
product range Sortiment
sample Probestück, Muster
staff Personal

Subject: **Re: Slimline update needed**

This is the current status:

· We have received the customer brochures from head office.
· Samples will be here by next week.
· There are still some open questions about pricing – we are waiting to hear back from head office.
· We have already put the training video for the sales team online.

That's all for now. I'll contact you again as soon as I have more information.

Martin

Dear Martin,

Can you update me on what's happening with the new product range? Do we have any samples yet? And what about the brochures?

Please let me know asap so I can start planning the training and info for the sales staff.

Thanks,
Graham

current status
(not ~~actual status~~)
= aktueller Stand

Which tasks are finished? Look at Martin's email again and tick the correct boxes.

- [ ] get new brochures
- [ ] decide on prices

- [ ] get samples
- [ ] put training video online

3 Read the update below. Is it all good news?
What is not ready yet? Discuss with a partner.

Vocabulary

behind schedule verspätet
currently derzeit, aktuell
to deliver liefern
to set a date einen Termin
   festlegen
translator Übersetzer/in

Subject: **Update – order and installation of packaging system**

Dear Zuzanna,

Just a quick email to update you on the current status of your order:

· Our technical team has finished the final testing of your packaging system.
· We are ready to deliver your order – it's currently with the logistics dept.
· We have set a date with your IT team for the installation of the system.
· Unfortunately, we are behind schedule with the documentation for your Czech staff. I'll speak
  with the translator and get back to you by the end of the week.

Regards,
Bernhard Deiser

---

4 Look at the emails in exercises 2 and 3 again and complete the phrases below.

> ### Phrases
>
> **Asking for and starting an update**
>
> Can you update me on .... [1] the new product range?
>
> Just a .... [2] the current status of your order: ...
>
> This is the situation at the moment: ...
>
> **Giving an update**
>
> We .... [3] the customer brochures from head office.
>
> Samples .... [4] by next week.
>
> We are .... [5] your order – it's .... [6] the logistics dept.
>
> Unfortunately, we are .... [7] with the documentation ...
>
> **Ending an update**
>
> I'll contact you again .... [8] I have more information.
>
> I'll speak with the translator and .... [9] by the end of the week.

5 Link items from the three columns to form sentences.

1 I'll contact you	the current	open questions.
2 The report	still some	I have more information.
3 We've	as soon as	with the brochures.
4 There are	behind schedule	status of the project.
5 This is	finished the	inbox by Friday.
6 We are	will be in your	training video.

Which of the sentences would you see at the a) beginning b) middle, and c) end of an update?

Did you know?

When giving an update, it's important to use the right verb form so that the status of the activities is clear to everybody.

> schon = already
> noch nicht = not ... yet

current activities:	future activities:	completed activities:
· We're (currently/still) **testing** the software.	· We **will test** the software (next week / soon).	· We've (already) **tested** the software. · We **haven't tested** the software (yet).

6 Complete the email with the correct form of the verbs.

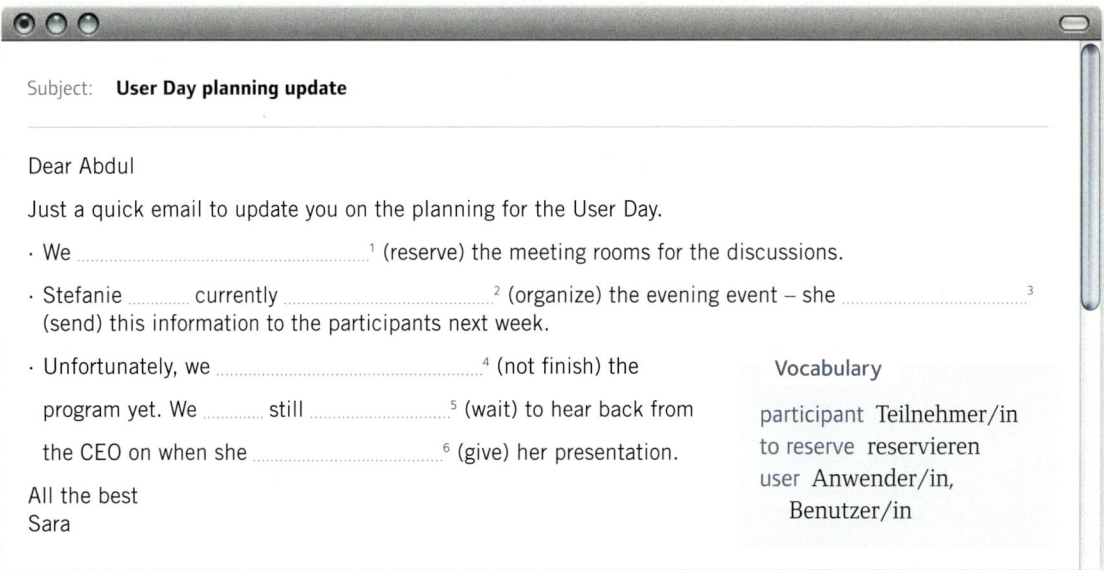

Subject: **User Day planning update**

Dear Abdul

Just a quick email to update you on the planning for the User Day.

- We _____¹ (reserve) the meeting rooms for the discussions.

- Stefanie _____ currently _____² (organize) the evening event – she _____³ (send) this information to the participants next week.

- Unfortunately, we _____⁴ (not finish) the program yet. We _____ still _____⁵ (wait) to hear back from the CEO on when she _____⁶ (give) her presentation.

All the best
Sara

Vocabulary

participant Teilnehmer/in
to reserve reservieren
user Anwender/in,
    Benutzer/in

Now complete these sentences so that they are true for you and tell a partner.

1 I am currently ...
2 I've already ...
3 I will ...
4 Unfortunately, we haven't ...
5 At the moment, ...
6 Next week, ...

7 ◁ 07 Helga and Antonio are discussing an IT project for a customer. Listen to the telephone call. Is it *all* bad news?

Listen again and find two mistakes in Helga's notes.

Antonio's call: IT Project Skywise

- two weeks behind schedule

- reason: system crash at another client's

- installation: have not set the date yet

- problems with our IT system – need to repair it before we can install software

- Andrea can do documentation

Vocabulary

crash Absturz
to repair sth. etw. reparieren

8 Read the email Antonio writes to Skywise. Does he *only* describe the problems? Discuss with a partner.

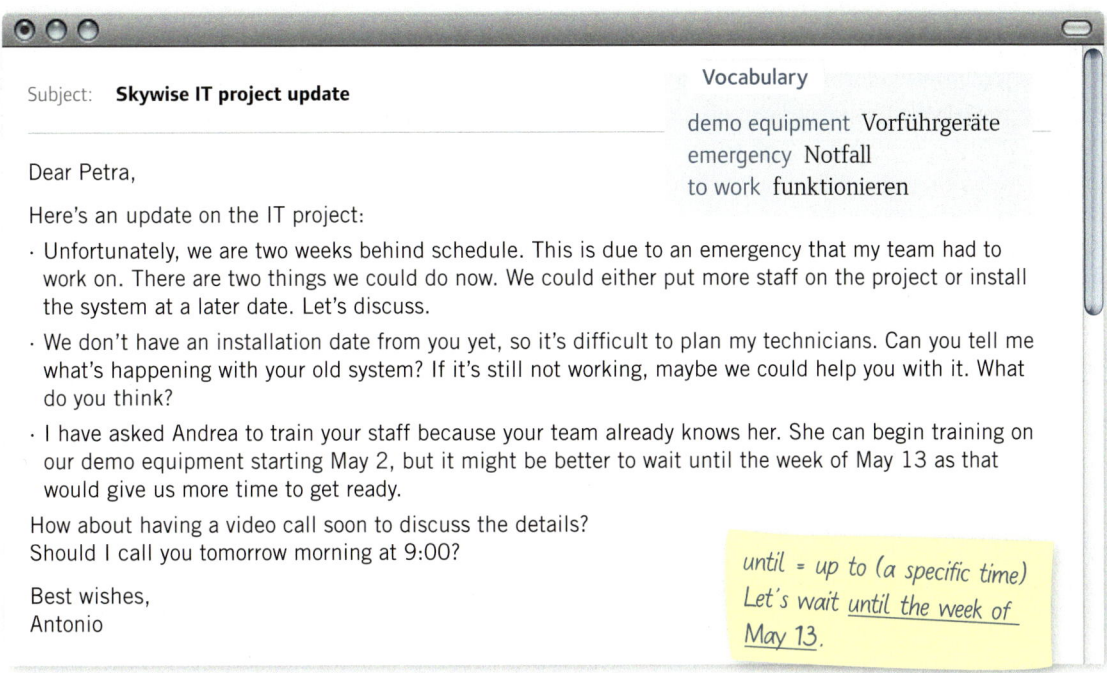

Subject: **Skywise IT project update**

Vocabulary

demo equipment Vorführgeräte
emergency Notfall
to work funktionieren

Dear Petra,

Here's an update on the IT project:

· Unfortunately, we are two weeks behind schedule. This is due to an emergency that my team had to work on. There are two things we could do now. We could either put more staff on the project or install the system at a later date. Let's discuss.

· We don't have an installation date from you yet, so it's difficult to plan my technicians. Can you tell me what's happening with your old system? If it's still not working, maybe we could help you with it. What do you think?

· I have asked Andrea to train your staff because your team already knows her. She can begin training on our demo equipment starting May 2, but it might be better to wait until the week of May 13 as that would give us more time to get ready.

How about having a video call soon to discuss the details?
Should I call you tomorrow morning at 9:00?

Best wishes,
Antonio

until = up to (a specific time)
Let's wait until the week of May 13.

9 Read the email again and complete the phrases below.

Phrases

Giving reasons

This is .... ¹ that my team had to work on.

We don't have an installation date from you yet, ... ² to plan my technicians.

I have asked Andrea to train your staff .... ³ your team already knows her.

Making suggestions

We could .... ⁴ on the project .... ⁵ the system at a later date.

If it's still not working, ... ⁶ help you with it.

.... ⁷ a video call soon to discuss the details?

---

10 Choose the correct words to complete the sentences.

1 The order will be late *due to / because* a problem with production.
2 We have a great team, *but / so* unfortunately we are still behind schedule with the project.
3 *Either / Or* we can send a technician *either / or* you can download our manual.
4 The results were not very good, *but / so* we stopped making the product.
5 The report isn't finished *because / due to* the results haven't arrived yet.
6 We know which products we need, *because / so* we are ready to place the order.

Key phrases

Here are some key phrases from the unit. Tick the ones that are useful for you.

Asking for an update
- Can you update me on what's happening with …?
- Can you tell me the current status of …?

Starting an update
- Just a quick email to update you on …
- This is the situation at the moment: …
- This is the current status: …
- Here's an update on …

Giving an update
- We have set a date with …
- Our team has finished …
- Unfortunately, we haven't finished … yet.
- We are behind schedule with …
- We are ready to …
- I am currently organizing …
- We are waiting to hear back from …
- Samples will be here by next week.
- I will send the information tomorrow.

Making suggestions
- We could either … or …
- If it is still not working, maybe we could …
- How about having …?
- Should I …?

Giving updates

Ending an update
- That's all for now.
- I'll contact you again as soon as I have more information.
- I'll get back to you by the end of the week.

Giving reasons
- This is due to …
- I have … because …
- We don't have …, so it's difficult to …

You will find an English–German list of these phrases on page 72.

Use this space to write your own useful words and phrases.

....

....

....

....

....

....

....

Over to you

11 **Prepare to update someone in an email.**

Who are you updating? **Name:** ....

What's the update about? **Subject line:** ....

List some of the things you …
a have already done: ....

b are doing at the moment: ....

c still need to do: ....

List any problems (and reasons for them) that connect to a, b, or c: ....

....

Make suggestions for some of the problems: ....

....

Now write an email using the information above and some of the key phrases opposite.

12 **Swap emails with a partner, then follow the steps below.**

1 Make a list of the things your partner a) has finished, b) is still working on, c) will do soon.
2 Do you have any questions about your partner's update? Ask for more information in a second email if anything is unclear.

Last but not least

13 **Read the tips on giving effective updates. Which tip do you find most useful?**

Tips for effective updates

- Make sure your update presents facts, and is clear and up to date. Use bullet points to make your report easy to read.

- How often you send updates is important. Sending a weekly status report to your team or client works best for most people. Some teams might only need updates every two weeks, but a month is usually too long to wait for information.

- Make a list of main achievements from this week (e.g. what I/we have done) and main activities for the next week (e.g. what I/we will do). This will help you stay motivated and on schedule.

- Some people like to use the "traffic light" system. Points that are marked red are "behind schedule", points that are marked yellow are "at risk", and points that are that are marked green are "on schedule". If any of the points in your update are red or yellow, you should make suggestions for how they can become green.

How do you give updates? Do you have any tips to add to the list? Are there any tips above that you want to try? Discuss with a partner.

Learning objectives
- Arranging appointments
  Termine vereinbaren
- Accepting and declining invitations
  Einladungen annehmen und ablehnen
- Changing appointments
  Termine verlegen

6 Making arrangements

---

1 Discuss with a partner.

! appointment = Termin
date = private Verabredung oder Datum

1 How often do you meet with colleagues or business partners?
2 Who usually arranges the appointments or meetings?
3 How do you usually make appointments? By email? By phone? Face to face?
4 Is your calendar often full? How easy is it to find a date and time for a meeting?

2 Two people are writing to arrange a meeting. Read the emails and complete the table.

who:	Matthias Brand	Anton Feistinger
when:		
where:		
why:		

Vocabulary

whatever egal welche
to be convenient for sb.
jdm. passen

1

Dear Matthias,

I hear you are going to the trade fair in Berlin next week. I'll also be there from Wednesday to Friday. Would you have time to meet for dinner? We could discuss the new project.

Would Thursday evening at 6:00 be OK for you? I think we are both staying at the Park Hotel, so we could eat at the restaurant there.

Let me know if that would work for you.

Best regards,
Sally

2

Dear Mr. Feistinger

It was nice meeting you at the trade fair.

We will be in Leipzig at the beginning of November and would like to meet to present our new product range to you and your team.

We are free on Tuesday, November 5, and could come to your office at whatever time is convenient for you.

I look forward to your reply.

Best wishes
Lionel Pellegrini

to meet = kennenlernen
It was nice meeting you.
to meet = treffen
Would you have time to meet?

How well do you think the writers know the people they are writing to? Discuss with a partner.

3 Now read the two replies and answer the questions.

1 Which person accepts the invitation?
2 Why does he suggest a new place to meet?
3 Why can't the other person meet?

Vocabulary

area Gegend
to suggest vorschlagen

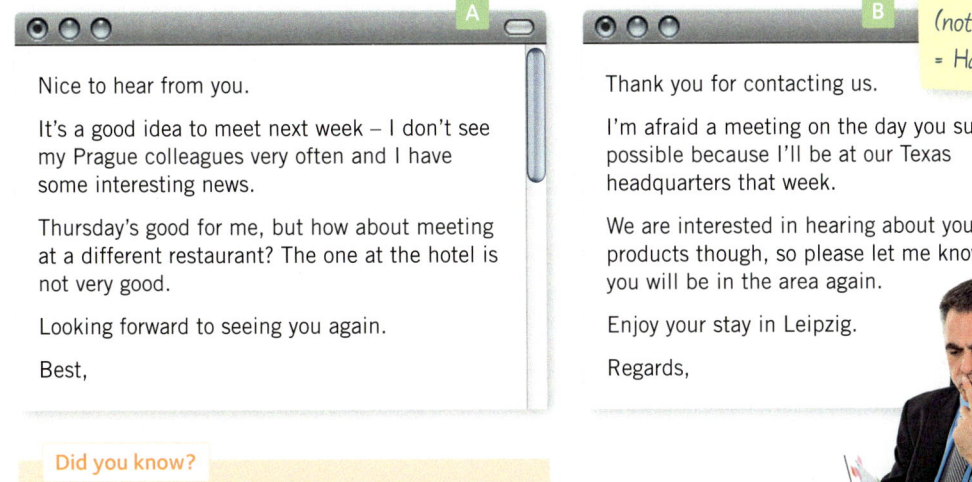

A

Nice to hear from you.

It's a good idea to meet next week – I don't see my Prague colleagues very often and I have some interesting news.

Thursday's good for me, but how about meeting at a different restaurant? The one at the hotel is not very good.

Looking forward to seeing you again.

Best,

B

Thank you for contacting us.

I'm afraid a meeting on the day you suggest isn't possible because I'll be at our Texas headquarters that week.

We are interested in hearing about your new products though, so please let me know when you will be in the area again.

Enjoy your stay in Leipzig.

Regards,

headquarters (not headquarter) = Hauptsitz

Did you know?

In less formal emails, people don't always write the first word or words of sentences like these:

(It's) Nice to hear from you.
(I'm) Looking forward to seeing you again.

4 Look at the emails in exercises 2 and 3 again and complete the phrases below.

Phrases

Arranging appointments

Would you ....¹ dinner?

Let me know if that would ....² you.

We … would like ....³ our new product range …

Suggesting a time and place

Would Thursday evening at 6:00 p.m. ....⁴?

We … could come to your office at whatever time ....⁵.

… but ....⁶ at a different restaurant?

Accepting or declining an invitation

Thursday's ....⁷ me …

I'm afraid a meeting on the day you suggest ....⁸ because …

5 Match the parts of the sentences.

1 Do you have time to meet for	the afternoon.
2 Can we meet on Monday? I'm free in	Tuesday afternoon.
3 Would Friday morning at	lunch tomorrow?
4 How about meeting at	9:00 be convenient?
5 I'm free on	the reception desk?

Now match sentences 1–5 to the replies below.

- ☐ a Three o'clock would work for me. See you on Monday.
- ☐ b Unfortunately, Tuesday won't work. How about Thursday?
- ☐ c Sorry, lunch isn't possible. I'm on a business trip all week.
- ☐ d Yes, let's meet there. Please call me when you arrive.
- ☐ e Friday a.m. is good for me. Looking forward to seeing you then.

Did you know?

The 24-hour clock is not used very often in the English-speaking world. It is better to use "a.m." or "p.m."

6:00 = 6:00 a.m.

18:00 = 6:00 p.m.

12:00 = noon (AE) / midday (BE)

24:00 = midnight

6 Look at some reasons for not accepting an invitation to meet, and add the missing prepositions.

at · at · from · in · on · on

I'm afraid Sorry, Unfortunately,	I'm	not .... [1] the office not .... [2] work .... [3] vacation working .... [4] home .... [5] a business trip .... [6] a client's (office)	today. this morning/afternoon. this week. all day/week.

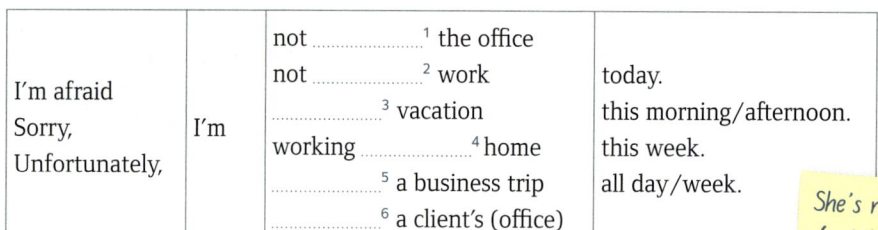

She's not in the office.
(not ~~She's not in the house.~~)
= Sie ist außer Haus.

👥 Which reasons from above have you used before? Tell a partner.

7 Complete the emails with the words below.

could we · fine for me · how about · like to · see you · unfortunately · work for you

Dear Christof

.... [1] meet on Wednesday at 10 am?

I'd .... [2] discuss the ideas for the new design. Please let me know.

Best
Jack

Hi Jack,

Thanks for your email. It's a good idea to meet.

.... [3], I won't be in the office on Wednesday morning.

.... [4] meeting in the afternoon? I could come to your office at around 2. Would that .... [5]?

Best,
Christof

Wednesday at 2 pm is .... [6].
.... [7] then.

Jack

Did you know?

Sometimes people write "am/pm" or "AM/PM" instead of "a.m./p.m."

8 It's Tuesday, and Jack writes another email. Why does he need to change his plans?

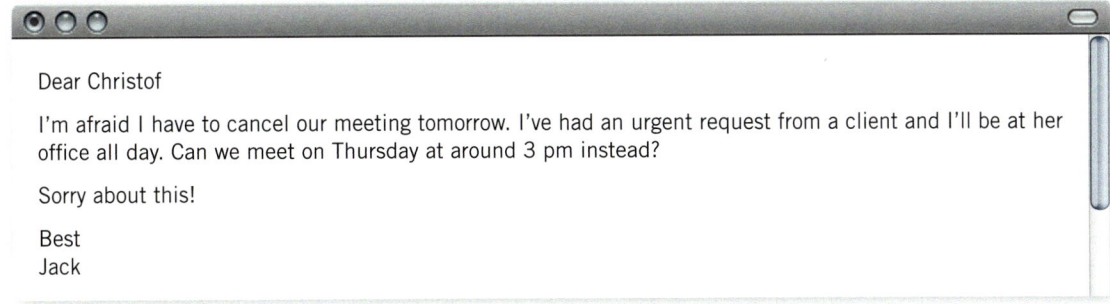

Dear Christof

I'm afraid I have to cancel our meeting tomorrow. I've had an urgent request from a client and I'll be at her office all day. Can we meet on Thursday at around 3 pm instead?

Sorry about this!

Best
Jack

Now look at the email below. What reason does Silke give for changing her plans?

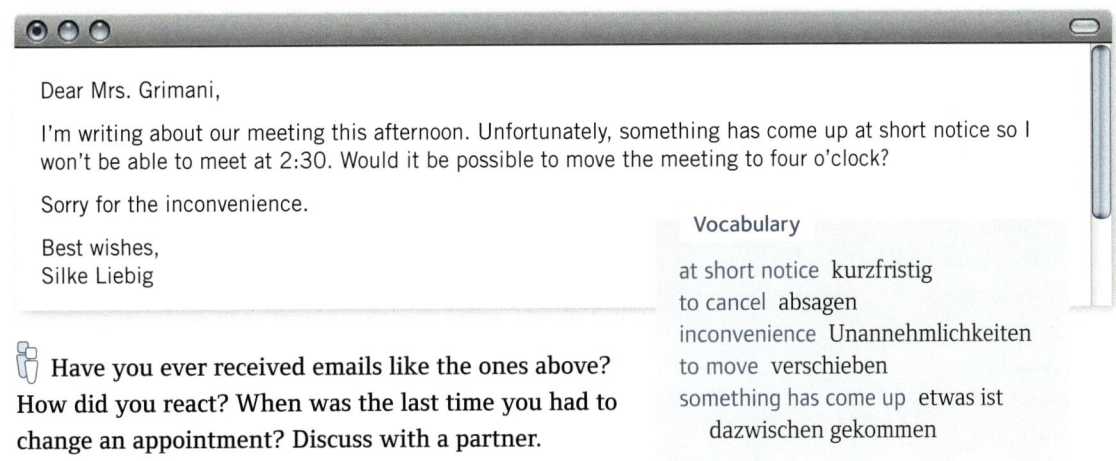

Dear Mrs. Grimani,

I'm writing about our meeting this afternoon. Unfortunately, something has come up at short notice so I won't be able to meet at 2:30. Would it be possible to move the meeting to four o'clock?

Sorry for the inconvenience.

Best wishes,
Silke Liebig

Vocabulary

at short notice kurzfristig
to cancel absagen
inconvenience Unannehmlichkeiten
to move verschieben
something has come up etwas ist
    dazwischen gekommen

Have you ever received emails like the ones above? How did you react? When was the last time you had to change an appointment? Discuss with a partner.

9 Look at the emails in exercise 8 again and complete the phrases below.

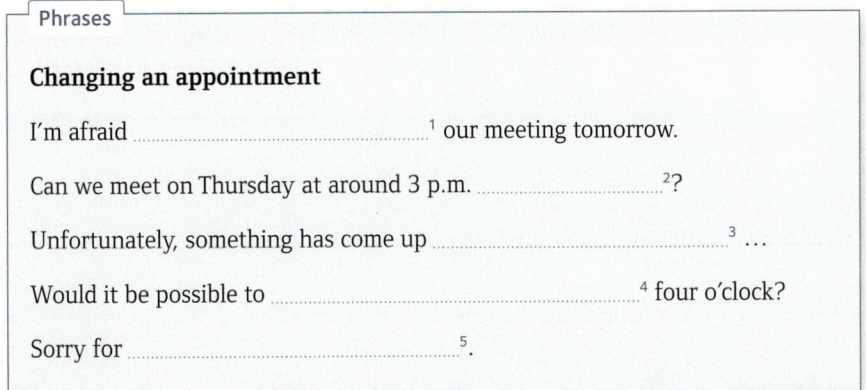

Phrases

Changing an appointment

I'm afraid ....¹ our meeting tomorrow.

Can we meet on Thursday at around 3 p.m. ....²?

Unfortunately, something has come up ....³ ...

Would it be possible to ....⁴ four o'clock?

Sorry for ....⁵.

10 ◁08 Something has come up and Amanda needs to change her plans. Listen and complete the sentences.

1 Miguel asks Amanda to …
2 Amanda has a meeting planned with … on …
3 She will …

Now use phrases from the unit to write the email for Amanda.

Here are some key phrases from the unit. Tick the ones that are useful for you.

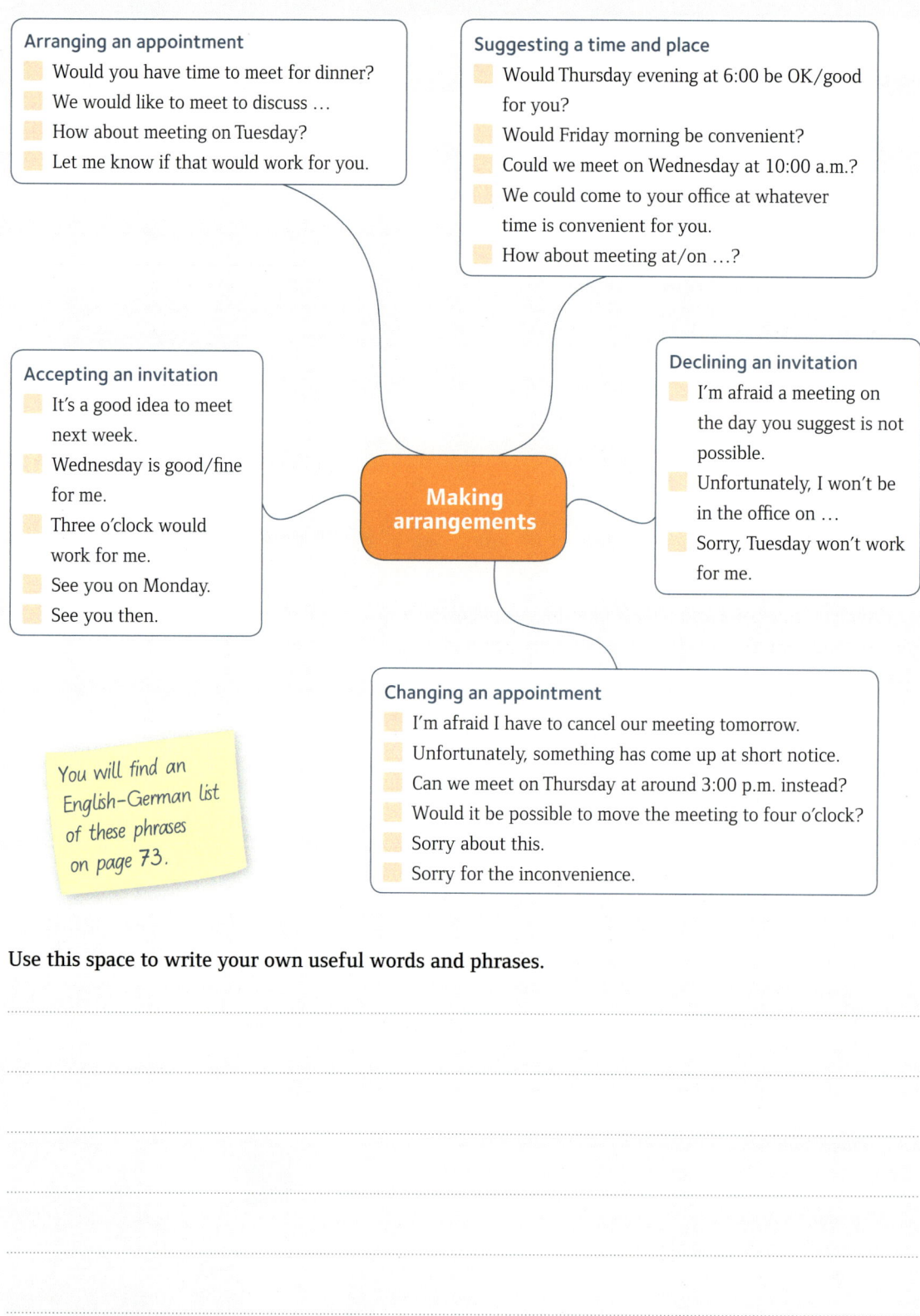

Arranging an appointment

Would you have time to meet for dinner?

We would like to meet to discuss …

How about meeting on Tuesday?

Let me know if that would work for you.

Suggesting a time and place

Would Thursday evening at 6:00 be OK/good for you?

Would Friday morning be convenient?

Could we meet on Wednesday at 10:00 a.m.?

We could come to your office at whatever time is convenient for you.

How about meeting at/on …?

Accepting an invitation

It's a good idea to meet next week.

Wednesday is good/fine for me.

Three o'clock would work for me.

See you on Monday.

See you then.

Making arrangements

Declining an invitation

I'm afraid a meeting on the day you suggest is not possible.

Unfortunately, I won't be in the office on …

Sorry, Tuesday won't work for me.

Changing an appointment

I'm afraid I have to cancel our meeting tomorrow.

Unfortunately, something has come up at short notice.

Can we meet on Thursday at around 3:00 p.m. instead?

Would it be possible to move the meeting to four o'clock?

Sorry about this.

Sorry for the inconvenience.

You will find an English–German list of these phrases on page 73.

Use this space to write your own useful words and phrases.

....

....

....

....

....

....

Over to you

11 Follow the steps below and use phrases from the opposite page to arrange a meeting with your partner.

> 1 Write an email to your partner to invite him or her to a meeting. Give the reason for the meeting and don't forget to include the time and place. Swap emails with your partner.

> 2 Reply to your partner's email, decline the invitation (give a good reason) and suggest another date or time. Swap emails with your partner.

> 3 Send a quick email to accept the new date or time. Swap emails with your partner.

> 4 Reply to the email. Something has come up. Cancel the meeting or try to find a new date or time. Swap emails with your partner.

> 5 Reply and swap emails with your partner.

Have you been able to arrange two meetings? When are you and your partner going to meet?

Last but not least

12 Read the tips below. Do you agree or disagree with them?
Do you have any tips to add to the list? Discuss with a partner.

CANCELLING AN APPOINTMENT

1 Let people know that you need to cancel as soon as you can. No one likes cancellations at short notice.

2 Always give a good reason why you need to cancel and make it clear that you are sorry for the inconvenience you have caused.

3 If possible, suggest a new date or time in the same email. This saves time. Suggest meeting at – or somewhere near – your colleague's or business partner's office, so meeting is easy for them.

4 If your calendars are connected with the same IT system, use the online calendar to request an appointment. This type of invitation is easy to accept or decline without a lot of emails back and forth.

Vocabulary

back and forth hin und her
cancellation Absage
to cause verursachen
near in der Nähe von
to save time Zeit sparen

near your colleague's office
(not ~~in the near of~~)

Learning objectives

· Checking and clarifying information
  Informationen überprüfen und klären

· Asking for confirmation
  Um Bestätigung bitten

· Correcting and confirming information
  Informationen korrigieren und
  bestätigen

7 | Checking information

1 Answer the questions for yourself, then compare your answers with a partner.

1 **When do you need to check or confirm information?**

☐ after a meeting ☐ after a phone call ☐ other ....

2 **What kind of information do you often need to clarify?**

☐ details of a meeting ☐ schedules

☐ figures ☐ who is responsible for what

☐ other ....

Vocabulary

figures Zahlen
schedule Zeitplan

2 Read the four emails. Which emails …

clarify information? .... ask for confirmation? ....

1

Hello Ingrid,

I'm writing the minutes of our meeting and there are a few points I'm not sure about. Can you please check the following?

· John will call (or email?) Meike T. about the payment.
· The report is due on Tuesday. (Or was that Thursday?)
· We are now over budget by €5,000. (Or €6,000?)
· We will change the deadline to Sept. 1. (Is that what we agreed?)

Thanks for your help.
Katy

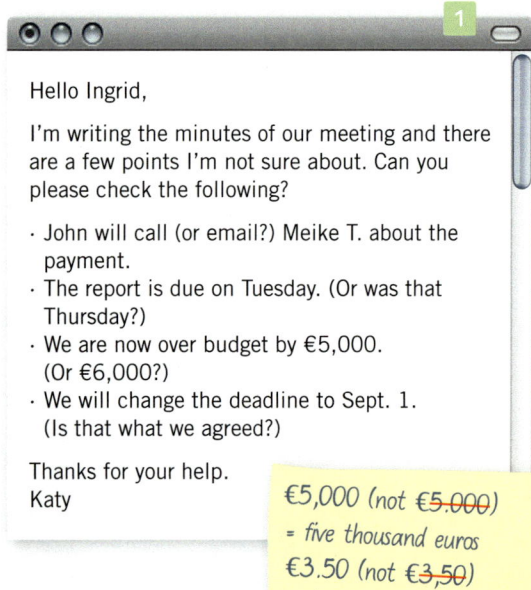

€5,000 (not ~~€5.000~~)
= five thousand euros
€3.50 (not ~~€3,50~~)
= three euros fifty

2

Dear Giovanni

Nice speaking to you yesterday. I think we clarified a lot of open points. Below is a summary of our telephone conversation.

· Training will take place in-house.
· Our technicians will just train key users so they can train their teams.
· We will supply manuals in Italian and English.

Please let me know if anything's incorrect or missing.

Best
Manuel

Vocabulary

to agree vereinbaren
by €5,000 um €5.000
in-house innerbetrieblich, intern
to supply liefern
to take place stattfinden

3

Marie,

I need to make sure I have all of Mr. Lee's travel details. See below:

Sunday, July 6: Arrival at 3:50 p.m. – taxi transfer to hotel
Monday, July 7: Taxi transfer to company at 9 a.m. (I've attached the schedule for meetings, etc.)
Tuesday, July 8: Departure at 10:15 a.m. – taxi transfer to airport at 7:30

Can you please confirm the above?

Thanks,
P

4

Just wanted to clarify what we spoke about yesterday in the kitchen.

Everybody in your department is going to the team-building workshop on Friday, right? Does that mean that no one will be in Accounting that day? If so, can you please send an email asap to let everyone in the company know? Thanks.

Vocabulary

arrival Ankunft
departure Abreise
kitchen (hier) Teeküche

Now match the emails to the subject lines below. Which subject lines are clear and effective? How can you make the others better? Discuss with a partner.

a ▨ Subject: Travel details
b ▨ Subject: Summary of discussion June 14
c ▨ Subject: Questions
d ▨ Subject: Team-building day – please inform staff

3 Look at the emails in exercise 2 again and complete the phrases below.

┌─ **Phrases** ───

Starting the email

I'm writing the minutes … and there are a few points .... [1].

Nice speaking to you yesterday. … Below is .... [2] our telephone conversation.

I need to .... [3] all of Mr. Lee's travel details. See below: …

.... [4] what we spoke about yesterday …

Checking and clarifying information

Can you please .... [5]?

The report is due on Tuesday. (Or .... [6] Thursday?)

We will change the deadline to Sept. 1. (Is that .... [7]?)

.... [8] that no one will be in Accounting that day?

Asking for confirmation

Please let me know if anything's .... [9].

Can you please .... [10]?

───

4 Complete the email with the words below.

agreed · get back · check · mean · points · summary · sure · was that

Here is a ....¹ of our discussion yesterday. There are a few ....² I'm not

........................³ about. Can you please ....⁴ and ....⁵ to me?

- Yanis will send us the test results by the end of the week. Is this what we ....⁶? Or the end of next week (the week of May 24)?

- We will report our results to the CTO before the group meeting in July. CTO (Chief Technical Officer) = Technischer Vorstand

  Or did you ....⁷ at the group meeting? Will the CTO be there?

- The quality assurance tests will begin on June 15, or ....⁸ July 15?

5 You want to send a summary of what was agreed at a meeting but are not sure about some points. With a partner, use the words in blue to clarify the information in the notes below.

1 The technician will train in-house. — our company? your company?

Did you mean in-house at our company or your company?

2 The product will cost $13. $30?

3 We will deliver the products to your plant. — in Poland or Ukraine?

— as PDF or by mail?

4 We will send the manual to you by the end of the week.

5 We need to finish the report by Wednesday. — 10th or 17th?

mit der Post = by mail (AE) = by post (BE)

6 Johanna writes to a colleague to clarify some points from a meeting. Read the email below. What does Ellen correct and what suggestion does she make?

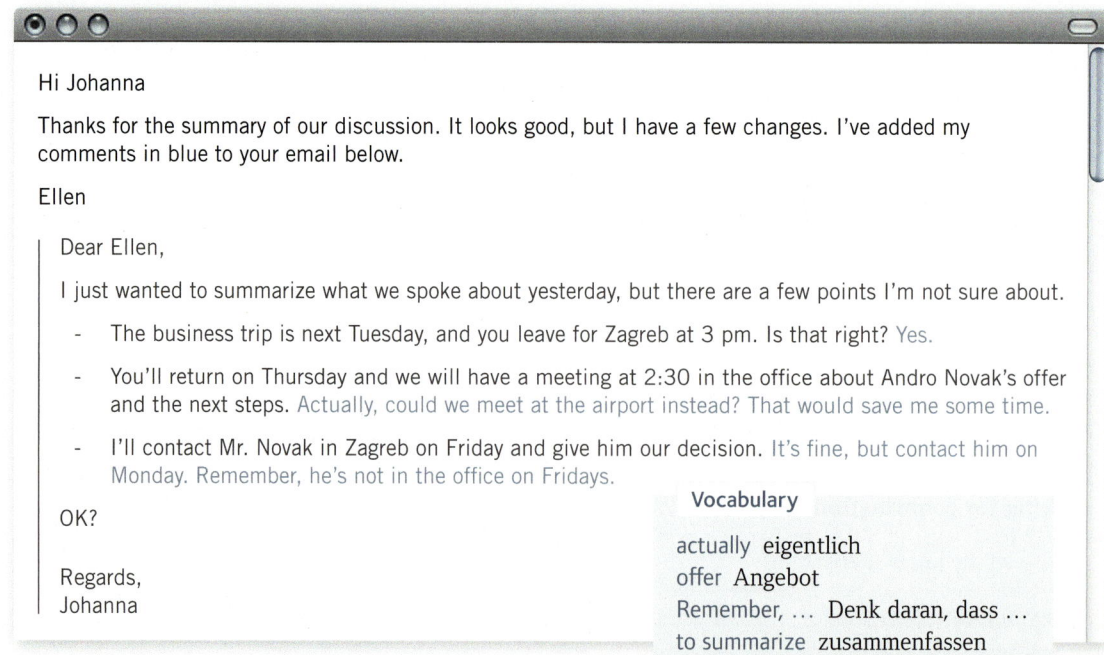

Hi Johanna

Thanks for the summary of our discussion. It looks good, but I have a few changes. I've added my comments in blue to your email below.

Ellen

Dear Ellen,

I just wanted to summarize what we spoke about yesterday, but there are a few points I'm not sure about.

- The business trip is next Tuesday, and you leave for Zagreb at 3 pm. Is that right? Yes.

- You'll return on Thursday and we will have a meeting at 2:30 in the office about Andro Novak's offer and the next steps. Actually, could we meet at the airport instead? That would save me some time.

- I'll contact Mr. Novak in Zagreb on Friday and give him our decision. It's fine, but contact him on Monday. Remember, he's not in the office on Fridays.

OK?

Regards,
Johanna

Vocabulary

actually eigentlich
offer Angebot
Remember, … Denk daran, dass …
to summarize zusammenfassen

7 Read the emails in exercise 6 again and complete the phrases below.

> **Phrases**
>
> **Correcting and confirming information**
>
> Thank you ....¹ our discussion.
>
> It looks good, but I have ....².
>
> I've just found a few mistakes.
>
> I've ....³ to your email below.
>
> ....⁴, could we meet at the airport instead?
>
> It's fine,...............⁵ contact him on Monday.
>
> I've read your summary and can confirm that everything is correct.

8 Match items from the three columns to form sentences.

1 I've added	to confirm	mistakes. See notes in red below.
2 Thank you	agreed to	to your email.
3 It looks good, but	my comments	deliver by June 16, not July.
4 It's fine,	for the notes	that everything's correct.
5 Actually, we	but	from our meeting.
6 I just wanted	I've found a few	the price is €13 (not 30).

9 Pierre's company is moving to a new building and he is unsure about some details. What does he need to clarify with Silvia?

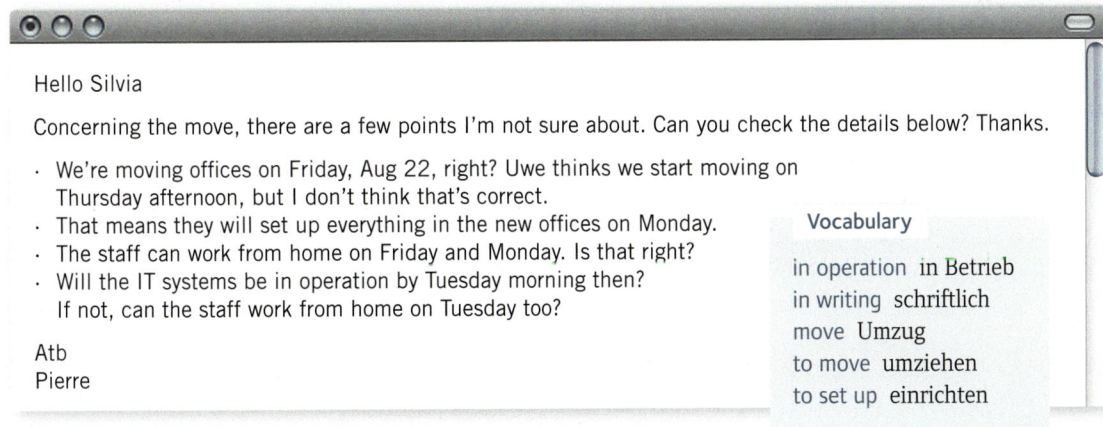

Hello Silvia

Concerning the move, there are a few points I'm not sure about. Can you check the details below? Thanks.

· We're moving offices on Friday, Aug 22, right? Uwe thinks we start moving on Thursday afternoon, but I don't think that's correct.
· That means they will set up everything in the new offices on Monday.
· The staff can work from home on Friday and Monday. Is that right?
· Will the IT systems be in operation by Tuesday morning then? If not, can the staff work from home on Tuesday too?

Atb
Pierre

Vocabulary

in operation in Betrieb
in writing schriftlich
move Umzug
to move umziehen
to set up einrichten

🔊09 Before Silvia can reply to Pierre's email, she sees him in the kitchen. Listen to their conversation. Does he now have answers to all of his questions? Why does Silvia offer to answer his questions in writing?

10 Write Sylvia's email. Confirm the information that is right and correct the information that is wrong.

You can start like this: *Thanks for your email. There are a few points to correct.*

Key phrases

Here are some key phrases from the unit. Tick the ones that are useful for you.

Starting the email
- [ ] I'm writing the minutes … and there are a few points I'm not sure about.
- [ ] Below is a summary of our telephone conversation.
- [ ] Here is a summary of our discussion …
- [ ] Just wanted to clarify what we spoke about yesterday …
- [ ] I need to make sure I have … . See below: …

Checking and clarifying information
- [ ] Can you please check the following?
- [ ] Can you check the details below?
- [ ] Or was that …?
- [ ] Or did you mean …?
- [ ] Is that what we agreed?
- [ ] Is that right?
- [ ] Does that mean that …?

Asking for confirmation
- [ ] Please let me know if anything's incorrect or missing.
- [ ] Can you please confirm the above / the following?

Checking information

Correcting and confirming information
- [ ] Thank you for the summary of our discussion.
- [ ] It looks good, but I have a few changes.
- [ ] Thank you for the notes from our meeting.
- [ ] I've just found a few mistakes.
- [ ] I've added my comments to your email below.
- [ ] Actually, …
- [ ] It's fine, but …
- [ ] I've read your summary and can confirm that everything is correct.

You will find an English–German list of these phrases on page 74.

Use this space to write your own useful words and phrases.

....

....

....

....

....

Over to you

11 With a partner, have a meeting to discuss the details of a current project or to make plans to go on a business trip together. Use the ideas in the word cloud for discussion points, or think of your own. Make notes on what you agree or decide.

....

....

....

....

> dates prices
> schedule **deadline**
> who is responsible for what
> **figures** next steps

Now write an email to summarize your discussion. Clarify the points you are unsure of or ask your partner to confirm that everything is correct. (If you wish, make some mistakes to see if your partner can find them!)

Swap emails with your partner and write a reply to confirm or correct the information in his or her email.

Last but not least

12 Read the article below. Which tips do you find the most useful? Can you add any tips of your own? Discuss with a partner.

> **Vocabulary**
>
> complicated kompliziert
> confusing unübersichtlich
> impression Eindruck
> typos Tippfehler

5 tips for clear communication

1 Make notes during meetings or phone calls. You might think you will remember everything, but most people don't. Good notes will also save you time when you are writing the minutes or sending a summary by email (see tip 3).

2 If you are meeting with colleagues, ask them to help summarize after a meeting or discussion. This will help make sure that everyone has understood the discussion in the same way.

3 It's helpful for everyone if you put the main points of a discussion in writing and send them to everyone who was at the meeting. If anything was unclear, you can clarify it with them right away.

4 Don't use complicated or technical language if the person you are writing to (or putting in cc) is not from your field.

5 Before you send an email, reread it and ask yourself: Is this clear for the reader? Rewrite anything that is confusing. This is also the time to check for mistakes. An email with a lot of typos might not be a problem when writing to colleagues, but it could make a bad impression on business partners.

8 Dealing with problems

1  **Tell your partner about a complaint you made or received recently.**

1 Was it by phone, face to face or in an email?
2 What was the complaint about?
3 How did you or the other person solve the problem, and were you both satisfied with the solution?

Vocabulary

complaint Beschwerde
satisfied zufrieden
to solve lösen

2 **Read the three complaints, and match them to the problem.**

a ▢ a printing mistake　　　b ▢ a late shipment　　　c ▢ the wrong information

---

○ ○ ○　　　　　　　　　　　　　　　　　　　　　　　1

Dear Ms. Trurow

I am writing to complain about a delay with our order. We ordered 100 Bestbuy S42 Tablets (order no. 25XCQ) on November 10, 20.. . According to the contract, the delivery date was November 22, so three days ago, but we have not received the shipment yet.

The delay is a problem for us, as we have had a lot of inquiries from customers and need the tablets urgently. Please let me know when the order will arrive.

Regards
Daniel Klepp

○ ○ ○　　　　　　　　　　　2

Hi Gerd

I'm afraid you sent me the wrong figures yesterday. I asked for the data on the Bentex product line, not the Tencho line. I need the info for the monthly report tomorrow, so please send it to me asap.

Thanks!
Stacy

Vocabulary

according to gemäß, nach
to complain sich
　beschweren
delay Verspätung
delivery date Liefertermin
printing Druck-
shipment Lieferung

Dear Inge,

This is to let you know that we are disappointed with the business cards we received this morning. The quality is good, but the color of the logo is not right. The logo should be dark blue, but it looks much lighter.

Can you please look into the matter and suggest a solution?

Best regards,
Patricia

Vocabulary

business cards Visitenkarten
disappointed enttäuscht
lighter heller
to look into the matter der Sache nachgehen

3 Look at the emails in exercise 2 again and complete the phrases below.

> **Phrases**
>
> **Making a complaint**
>
> I am writing ....[1] with our order.
>
> I am afraid you sent me the ....[2] yesterday.
>
> This is to let you know that ....[3] with the business cards …
>
> **Asking for action**
>
> Please ....[4] when the order will arrive.
>
> Can you please ....[5] and suggest ....[6]?
>
> Could you please tell me how we should proceed?

Vocabulary

to proceed vorgehen

4 Complete the two complaints with the words below.

> complain · contact · disappointed · look into ·
> lower · proceed · satisfied · short notice

I am ....[1] with the poor service we received today. We had an appointment with one of your technicians this morning, but she cancelled at very ....[2]. A second technician came in the afternoon but left after 15 minutes, and the machine still doesn't work.

Can you please ....[3] the matter and ....[4] me asap?

I'm writing to ....[5] about the brochures we ordered from you. We are not ....[6] with the quality. We asked for the "professional" quality (product no. GP 125), but you sent us the basic version on ....[7]-quality paper.

Could you please tell me how we should ....[8]?

5 Use the notes below to write an urgent email.

- *E-Mail an Milan Van Dijk*
- *Training fängt morgen Nachmittag an – Handbücher noch nicht angekommen!*
- *Wann hat er sie verschickt?*
- *Er soll der Sache nachgehen + so bald wie möglich Bescheid geben, was wir tun können*

6 Look back at exercise 2. With a partner, discuss how you would reply to the three emails. What solutions would you offer?

Now read the emails below. Are the replies and solutions similar to your ideas?

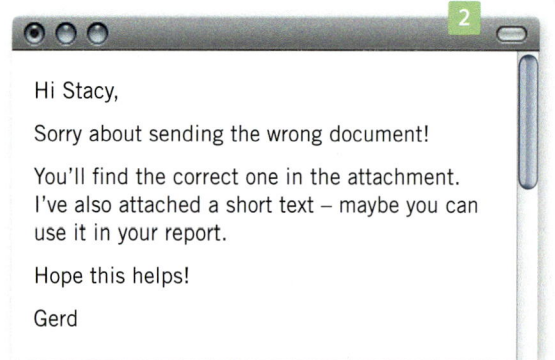

Dear Mr. Klepp,

Thank you for your email. We apologize for the delay in delivery. Unfortunately, we had a problem last week with our suppliers. We have checked the status of your order, and you should receive the shipment on December 2.

We apologize for the inconvenience.

If you need further help with your order, please call me at 0800 535 636.

Regards,
Jane Trurow

Hi Stacy,

Sorry about sending the wrong document!

You'll find the correct one in the attachment. I've also attached a short text – maybe you can use it in your report.

Hope this helps!

Gerd

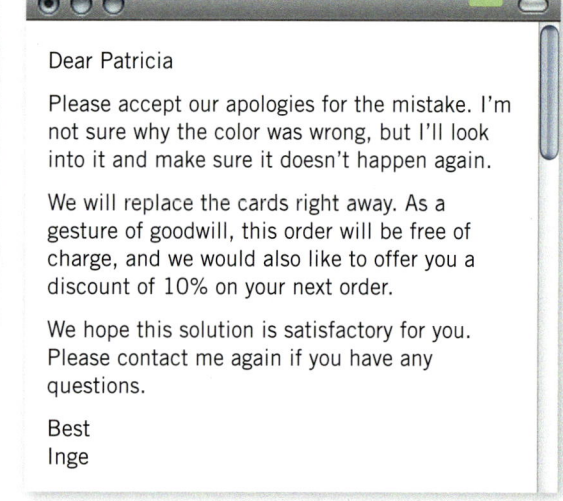

Dear Patricia

Please accept our apologies for the mistake. I'm not sure why the color was wrong, but I'll look into it and make sure it doesn't happen again.

We will replace the cards right away. As a gesture of goodwill, this order will be free of charge, and we would also like to offer you a discount of 10% on your next order.

We hope this solution is satisfactory for you. Please contact me again if you have any questions.

Best
Inge

7 Look at the emails in exercise 6 again and complete the phrases below.

Phrases

Apologizing

We ....[1] the delay in delivery.

....[2] sending the wrong document.

Please ....[3] for the mistake.

Offering solutions

We ....[4] the cards right away.

As a ....[5], this order will be ....[6],

and we would also like to ....[7] of 10% on your next order.

Ending the apology

We hope this solution is ....[8].
We hope you are satisfied with this solution.
Hope this helps!

---

8 Put the email below into the correct order. Why did the client complain, and what solution does Paula offer the client?

Dear Ms. Reed

☐ a This was due to illness and we are looking into the matter.

☐ b We hope you are satisfied with this solution.

☐ c Please let me know if that is convenient for you.

☐ d Please accept our apologies for cancelling the installation date at such short notice.

☐ e I have looked at the schedule and we can install the system next Monday.

☐ f As a gesture of goodwill, we would also like to offer you a 10% discount on the installation service.

Best regards
Paula Hirsch

👥 Discuss what solutions your company offers to deal with complaints.

9 🔊 10 Axel and Katya from AVS GmbH are deciding how to reply to a complaint. Listen and tick the correct boxes.

1 AVS GmbH ☐ overcharged Techtoys ☐ sent Techtoys the wrong order ☐.

2 Techtoys received an invoice for ☐ €8,350 ☐ €8,530 ☐.

3 Techtoys ☐ has already paid ☐ does not want to pay ☐ the invoice.

4 The reason for the mistake might be ☐ new staff ☐ the change to a new accounting system ☐.

5 Axel and Katya decide to ☐ refund the difference ☐ refund the whole amount ☐.

6 They also want to offer Techtoys a discount of ☐ five ☐ ten ☐ percent on their next order.

👥 Work with a partner and write Axel's email to Stella Alquist.

Key phrases

Here are some key phrases from the unit. Tick the ones that are useful for you.

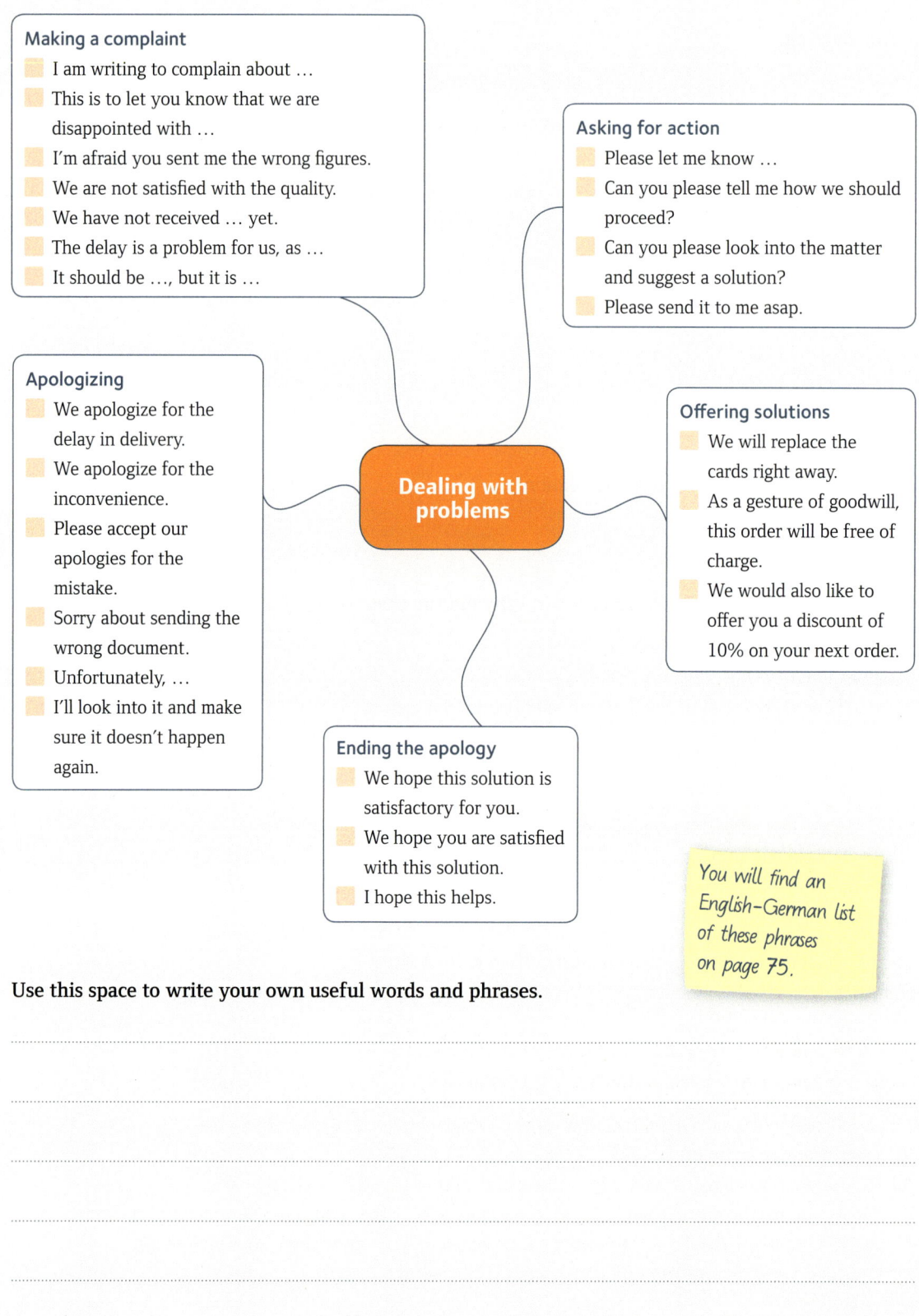

Making a complaint
- I am writing to complain about …
- This is to let you know that we are disappointed with …
- I'm afraid you sent me the wrong figures.
- We are not satisfied with the quality.
- We have not received … yet.
- The delay is a problem for us, as …
- It should be …, but it is …

Asking for action
- Please let me know …
- Can you please tell me how we should proceed?
- Can you please look into the matter and suggest a solution?
- Please send it to me asap.

Apologizing
- We apologize for the delay in delivery.
- We apologize for the inconvenience.
- Please accept our apologies for the mistake.
- Sorry about sending the wrong document.
- Unfortunately, …
- I'll look into it and make sure it doesn't happen again.

Dealing with problems

Offering solutions
- We will replace the cards right away.
- As a gesture of goodwill, this order will be free of charge.
- We would also like to offer you a discount of 10% on your next order.

Ending the apology
- We hope this solution is satisfactory for you.
- We hope you are satisfied with this solution.
- I hope this helps.

You will find an English–German list of these phrases on page 75.

Use this space to write your own useful words and phrases.

....

....

....

....

....

Over to you

10 Think about a complaint you or your department made recently and make notes below:

1 Who was the complaint sent to? ....

2 What did you complain about? ....

3 What action did you ask for? ....

Use your notes and the phrases opposite to write the complaint in English.

11 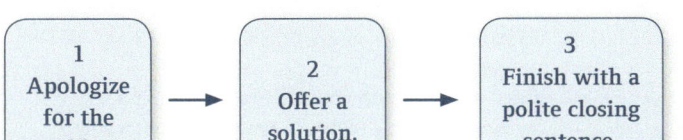 Swap emails and reply to your partner's complaint. Follow the steps below.

```
┌──────────────┐      ┌──────────────┐      ┌──────────────┐
│      1       │      │      2       │      │      3       │
│  Apologize   │ ───▶ │   Offer a    │ ───▶ │ Finish with a│
│   for the    │      │  solution.   │      │polite closing│
│  problem.    │      │              │      │  sentence.   │
└──────────────┘      └──────────────┘      └──────────────┘
```

Discuss your email with your partner. Were they satisfied with your apology and the solution you offered?

Last but not least

12 Read the comments on the chat forum called "Business dos and don'ts". Which opinions do you agree with?
What comments would you add? Discuss with a partner.

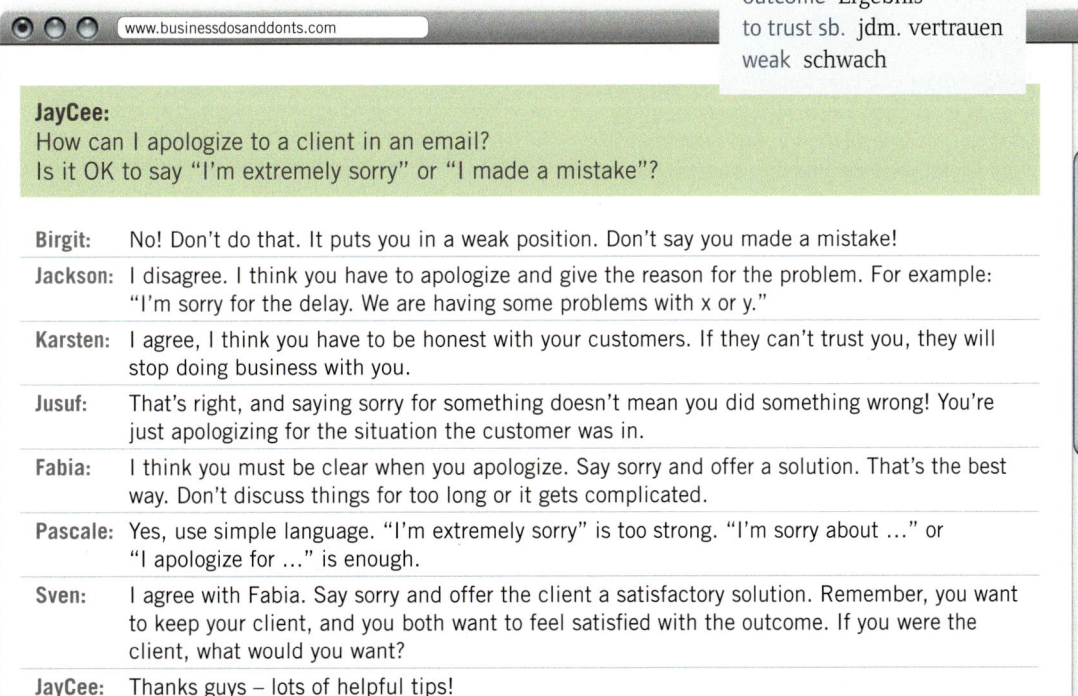

Vocabulary

honest ehrlich
to keep sb. jdn. halten
outcome Ergebnis
to trust sb. jdm. vertrauen
weak schwach

www.businessdosanddonts.com

JayCee:
How can I apologize to a client in an email?
Is it OK to say "I'm extremely sorry" or "I made a mistake"?

Birgit:	No! Don't do that. It puts you in a weak position. Don't say you made a mistake!
Jackson:	I disagree. I think you have to apologize and give the reason for the problem. For example: "I'm sorry for the delay. We are having some problems with x or y."
Karsten:	I agree, I think you have to be honest with your customers. If they can't trust you, they will stop doing business with you.
Jusuf:	That's right, and saying sorry for something doesn't mean you did something wrong! You're just apologizing for the situation the customer was in.
Fabia:	I think you must be clear when you apologize. Say sorry and offer a solution. That's the best way. Don't discuss things for too long or it gets complicated.
Pascale:	Yes, use simple language. "I'm extremely sorry" is too strong. "I'm sorry about ..." or "I apologize for ..." is enough.
Sven:	I agree with Fabia. Say sorry and offer the client a satisfactory solution. Remember, you want to keep your client, and you both want to feel satisfied with the outcome. If you were the client, what would you want?
JayCee:	Thanks guys – lots of helpful tips!

Transcripts

Unit 1   **Exercise 3**   🔊 02

1 I've checked my inbox and I have five new emails.
2 I'll forward your email to my colleague who is responsible for international orders.
3 I'm sending you our price list as an attachment.
4 Please cc Fritz and Sanjay so they also know about the changes.
5 This is an out of office message. I am on vacation until August 3 and will reply to your email when I return.
6 Please delete my last email. I sent you the wrong information.

Unit 1   **Exercise 8**   🔊 03

Justin Hello.
Gabriela Hello, Justin. This is Gabriela from Marketing.
Justin Hi, Gabi. So, are you going to sign up for the safety training course? I sent an email to everyone in your department last week.
Gabriela Yes, I got your email, but I'm not sure if I am interested. It sounds useful, but the problem is that I've just returned from vacation and I have so much work to do.
Justin Oh, I know the problem. I'm going on vacation at the end of August and it'll be the same for me when I get back. Well, think about it, but let me know soon.
Gabriela I'll contact you later today. I need to finish reading my emails and I also need to speak to my team leader first. She might say no if a lot of people from our department are already going. Oh, there she is. I'll talk to her now. Bye, Justin.
Justin OK. Bye.

Unit 2   **Exercise 6**   🔊 04

Gary Gary Taylor.
Martin Hi Gary, Martin here.
Gary Oh, hi Martin.
Martin I'm calling about the email I sent you.
Gary I'm sorry, I just got off the plane. I haven't checked my emails yet.
Martin Oh, that's right. You're in Paris this week. Yes, well, I need the details about the contact you made at the trade fair.
Gary Ah, the contact, right. Her name is Antonia Barker. I think I have her business card with me. Wait a minute … here it is. Do you have a pen?
Martin Err, yes.

Gary So, her email address is – antonia dot barker, that's A-N-T-O-N-I-A, dot B-A-R-K-E-R.
Martin Parker?
Gary No, Barker. B as in Berlin.
Martin Oh, Barker. OK. Antonia dot Barker …
Gary … at uniflex hyphen inc dot com. That's U-N-I-F-L-E-X hyphen I-N-C dot com.
Martin Uniflex …
Gary hyphen – or dash – I-N-C dot com.
Martin Oh, I see. Uniflex dash I-N-C dot com. OK, I've got that.
Gary Good. When you write to her, can you tell her something for me? She asked about a good restaurant in Amsterdam. Tell her it's called Daalder – D-A-A-L-D-E-R.
Martin Daalder. OK, I'll do that. Thanks and have a good trip, Gary.
Gary Thanks. Bye.
Martin Bye.

Unit 3   **Exercise 9**   🔊 05

Thomas Thomas Bieber, Guten Tag.
Alina Hi, Thomas. It's Alina here from the Bucharest plant.
Thomas Oh, hello Alina. How are you?
Alina Fine, thanks. Thomas, we need some information from you. Can you send me the results of the tests you did on the new 150 ml bottles? We want to use the bottles for a new product.
Thomas The 150 ml bottles. Yes, that's no problem. The test results were very good, by the way.
Alina Great. And another thing. We had a meeting last week and we decided to change our working times here. We want to use the shifts you have in Germany.
Thomas I see.
Alina So, could you send me a copy of your shift planner? You know, the planner you use to say who works in which shift? I'd like to see how you plan your team.
Thomas Sure. We have a program for that on the computer. I can send you a link – it's on our internal system.
Alina Thanks, that would be a big help. Uhm, Thomas, can you send me everything today? I'm going on vacation next week and have a lot to do.
Thomas No problem. I'll send you everything this afternoon.
Alina Great, thanks. Bye, Thomas.
Thomas Bye.

Exercise 9 ◁06

Bob So Karina, what's happening with Baxwell?

Karina Well, they want to place an order. A large one.

Bob That sounds good. So what's the problem?

Karina They haven't paid their last invoice. It's still outstanding.

Bob Oh. When was it due?

Karina Let me see. Invoice 201614 … it was due three weeks ago.

Bob Oh dear.

Karina Yes, and the accounting department wants payment before production starts working on their order.

Bob I see. OK. Let's write an email to … uhm … to John Leach – you know John, right?

Karina Yes, I do.

Bob Good, so tell him that the payment is urgent and we need to receive the money before we can start working on their order. I know John. He'll make sure that we get the payment asap. Tell him to contact one of us if he has any questions.

Karina OK, good. I'll write to him now and put you in cc.

Exercise 7 ◁07

Helga Good morning, Antonio.

Antonio Morning, Helga. How are you this morning?

Helga Fine, thanks. And you?

Antonio Not bad. Um, do you have a minute?

Helga Sure. What can I help you with?

Antonio Well, I'm calling about the IT project for our client Skywise.

Helga Ah, good. How's it going?

Antonio Good and bad! I want to update you on some points before I contact the client.

Helga OK.

Antonio First of all, we are two weeks behind schedule. My IT team had to work on a system crash at another client's.

Helga Two weeks. That's not good.

Antonio I know, but my team has finished there now and they're ready to work on the Skywise project again.

Helga That's good. When will you install the new system there?

Antonio Unfortunately, I have no idea. Petra at Skywise hasn't sent us any dates yet.

Helga Why not?

Antonio Well, they said they have problems with their IT system. And we can't install anything new if their system isn't working.

Helga No, of course not. Anything else?

Antonio Yes, but good news!

Helga Oh, that's good to hear.

Antonio I've spoken to Andrea and she can do the training for them. They know her because she's trained there before, so Petra will be happy to hear that.

Helga Great. So what will you tell Petra about the other things?

Antonio Well, I'll email her first and …

Exercise 10 ◁08

Miguel Ah, Amanda. Do you have a minute?

Amanda Yeah, sure.

Miguel I'm afraid we need you to go on a business trip to Geneva next week to see how the new project is going.

Amanda Oh, but I have an appointment on Tuesday – an important one, with Mark Jones from Great Foods.

Miguel Sorry, you'll have to cancel it. The visit to Geneva is urgent and much more important.

Amanda But it's such short notice. Mark is not going to be happy.

Miguel I know, but I'm sure you can find another time to meet with him.

Amanda OK, I'll email him and suggest another date.

Miguel Great. Thanks, Amanda.

Exercise 9 ◁09

Silvia Oh, hi Pierre. You're getting a coffee too, I see.

Pierre Yes. It's that time of day!

Silvia Yes, I know.

Pierre Did you see my email about the move?

Silvia Yes, I did. I started to answer it, but then decided to get a cup of coffee first.

Pierre So, did I have the right date? The move is on Friday, the 22nd?

Silvia Yes, that's right. They move everything on Friday.

Pierre OK. And what about the staff? That means they can work from home on Friday, right? And Monday too?

Silvia Well, Friday yes. Some of the IT staff will need to come to work and help with the computer network, but the normal office staff can work from home. But only on Friday. Everybody needs to be back at work on Monday.

Pierre Oh, OK. I thought they could work from home on Monday, and maybe Tuesday too if things aren't set up yet.

Silvia No, the first working day in the new office is Monday, the 25th.

Pierre But are you sure the computer network will be working then? Will we be able to get and send emails, for example?

Silvia Yes, it should be working by then. The IT staff will work over the weekend to set up everything.

Pierre OK. I think I understand now. So, just to make sure, the move is on Friday, but …

Silvia Listen, Pierre, I already started to answer your email so why don't I just finish it now? Would that help? Then you will have all the correct information in writing.

Pierre Yes, that would be a big help. Thanks, Silvia.

Silvia No problem. Now that I have my coffee, that is.

| Unit 8 | **Exercise 9** | ◁ 10 |

Katya Hello.

Axel Hi Katya, this is Axel. Do you have a minute?

Katya Sure.

Axel I've just spoken to Stella Alquist – she works in the accounting department at Techtoys.

Katya OK.

Axel Well, she wrote to us and complained that we overcharged them for their last order.

Katya Is she right? Was the invoice too high?

Axel Yes, unfortunately, she's right. The order was for €8,350, but the amount on the invoice was €8,530, so a difference of 180 euros. And the other thing is, they paid the invoice before they saw it was wrong.

Katya I see. I wonder how the mistake happened. When did we send the invoice?

Axel Let me see … the date on the invoice is May 23rd.

Katya Well, that was when we changed to the new accounting system, wasn't it?

Axel Ah yes, you're right. And I know the accounting staff was very busy then.

Katya Right. OK, so send them an email and apologize. And tell them we will refund the difference asap of course.

Axel Of course, but is there anything else we can do? They're a big client so we want them to be happy. And, remember, we had those problems a few months ago.

Katya Ah yes, right. OK, let's offer them something "as a gesture of goodwill"?

Axel How about a discount on their next order?

Katya Yes, that's a good idea. Offer them five percent.

Axel OK, I'll write to Stella right now.

Katya Great. Thanks, Axel.

Axel Thank you, Katya. Goodbye.

Katya Bye.

Answer key

Unit 1

Exercise 1 (open answer)

Exercise 2

attachment	6
drafts	4
folders	5
high priority	8
inbox	1
outbox	2
sent	3
subject	7

send & receive	a
delete	e
cc	g
print	f
reply	b
reply all	c
forward	d

Exercise 3
1 inbox
2 forward
3 attachment
4 cc
5 reply
6 delete

Exercise 4
(model answers)
1 f 2 c 3 d 4 a 5 e 6 b

Exercise 5
1 b 2 d 3 c 4 f

Exercise 6
1 I'm writing **about** the training course …
2 **Concerning** the meeting last week, …
3 I am writing to **inquire about** a summer job …
4 I'm **contacting you about** Johanna.
5 I **hope you had** a good vacation.
6 I **look forward to hearing** from you.

Exercise 7
1 d 2 f 3 a 4 b 5 e 6 c

Exercise 8
Gabriele calls about email number 1. She wants to know more about the course because she is not sure she has time for it. She also needs to talk to her team leader.
1 speaking to you
2 sign me up for the course
3 it will be useful
4 team leader
5 Thanks!

Exercise 9
1 Thank you *(remember, capital letter!)*
2 forwarding
3 responsible
4 contacting
5 let you know
6 Concerning *(remember, capital letter!)*
7 attached

1 c 2 a 3 b

Exercises 10–12 (open answers)

Unit 2

Exercise 1 (open answers)

Exercise 2
a 2 contact information
b 3 times or dates
c 1 rules and regulations
d 4 personal information

Exercise 3 (open answers)

Exercise 4
1 Could you **please let me know** about my contract …
2 I'd like **some information about** the new client.
3 Can you please send it **as an attachment** to me?
4 **Please send me** your vacation plans for Christmas.
5 I **received your name from** your colleague in the HR department.
6 **I work in** the sales department and …

Exercise 5
a Could you please send it as an attachment
b Can you give me more information about
c I received your name from my colleague
d I need the manual
e We need to update our system

1 b
2 e
3 c
4 d
5 a

Exercise 6
(model answer)
Gary asks Martin to tell Antonia Barker the name of a restaurant in Amsterdam.

1 Antonia Barker <antonia.barker@uniflex-inc.com>
2 Dear Ms. Barker
3 Daalder

Exercise 7

1 with information about himself
2 a price

1 I **am the** Head Technician at Antco AG …
2 … **based in** Dortmund.
3 My colleague gave **me your contact details.**
4 I'm **inquiring about** the packaging machinery your company produces.
5 We **are interested in** the SYG9 model.

Exercise 8

more formal (for first contacts)	neutral (for colleagues)
Thank you	Thanks
Could you please tell us …?	Can you let us know …?
to inquire about sth.	to ask about sth.
to purchase	to buy
We are interested in getting …	We need to get …
to request sth.	to ask for sth.

Exercise 9

1 My name is Andreas Hayek
2 I am contacting
3 we are interested in purchasing
4 Could you please
5 Thank you in advance.
6 Best regards

Exercise 10
(model answer)

1 Dear Ms. Armstrong (or Mrs. Armstrong if you know that she is married)
2 I am a technician at Media Systems.
3 I received your name from your colleague in the Berlin office.
4 I am contacting you because we are interested in your quality tests.
5 Could you please send us the results as an attachment?
6 Thank you in advance.
7 Best wishes / Best regards

Exercises 11 + 12 (open answers)

Unit 3

Exercise 1 (open answers)

Exercise 2
a 2 b 3 c 1 d 4

(model answers)

a Emails 2 and 3 are replying to a colleague or someone the writer knows.

email 2 Anke doesn't start her email with a greeting and she only uses an initial (A for Anke) as a close. She also writes "See you at the meeting next week", so they are probably colleagues in the same department or office.

email 3 Philippe uses Conny's first name and says it is nice to hear from her again. This email is more formal than email 2, so they probably don't know each other very well. He talks about "our" Toulouse factory so maybe they are business partners.

b 1 and 4 are emails to a first-time contact.

email 1 Nigel uses a last name in the greeting and a first and last name in the close, and the language in the email is formal.

email 4 Sergei's email is less formal than email 1 but he probably doesn't know Michael because there is no personal language. We don't know 100%, but Laura could be Michael's colleague and she gave him Sergei's contact information.

Exercise 3

1 Thank you for **your interest in** our products.
2 **Regarding** the vacation dates you need, …
3 **Thanks for your** email – it's nice to hear from you again.
4 Please find our PDF **brochure in the attachment.**
5 I've **attached a** spreadsheet with …
6 You can use **the link below** to find a full description of …
7 Please contact me if you **have further questions.**
8 **Let me know if** you have any more questions.
9 I'd be **glad to give you** a demonstration …
10 Feel free **to contact me** if you need anything else.

Exercise 4
1
I am attaching the price list you wanted.
You can use the link below to download the brochure.
Please find the information attached.

2
We would be glad to send you more information.
Feel free to contact me if you have further questions.

3
Thank you for your interest.
Thank you for contacting me.

a 3 b 1 c 2

Exercise 5
1 a 2 b 3 a 4 b 5 a

Exercise 6
Mr. Schöberl needs to complete a questionnaire and send it to Ms. Peruzzi. His reply should be formal.
Sandra needs to write a short report (in German or English) on a seminar that she attended and send it to Jon. Her reply can be less formal.

Exercise 7
1
1 d 2 a 3 c 4 b

2
1 b 2 d 3 c 4 a 5 e

Exercise 8
1 e.g. (= z. B. / zum Beispiel)
2 info
3 fyi, sometimes FYI (= zur Information)
4 etc. (= usw.)
5 re (= betreffs)
6 dept. (= Abt./Abteilung)
7 atb, sometimes ATB
8 btw (= übrigens)

Exercise 9
Alina is calling from the Bucharest plant. Yes, she knows Thomas.
She wants the test results on the 150 ml bottles and a copy of the shift planner.

Exercise 10
(model answer)
Dear Alina,
It was nice speaking to you this morning.
I've attached the test results that you asked for.
Regarding the shift planner you need, you can use the link below.
(link)
Feel free to contact me if you have any more questions.
Have a good vacation!
Best,
Thomas

Exercise 11 (open answer)

Exercise 12
1 d 2 e 3 a 4 c 5 b 6 (open answer)

Unit 4
....

Exercises 1 (open answers)

Exercise 2
a 2 agenda points
b 3 payment
c 1 customer information

Exercise 3
1 This is **a gentle** reminder.
2 We **need to update** our customer contacts.
3 This is **to let you know that** invoice no. … is outstanding.
4 Please **check the list attached** and update anything that isn't correct.
5 Could you please **send me your points** for the agenda asap?
6 Please **transfer the payment** by April 30, 20.. .
7 I need the list back **by the end of** the week so we can meet the deadline.
8 I need them **by Friday at the latest.**

Exercise 4
1 c 2 e 3 a 4 b 5 d

opening sentences: 1c, 4b, 5d
requests: 2e, 3a

Exercise 5
1 on Friday
2 by
3 a month ago
4 by
5 by Wednesday, on
6 five days ago

Exercise 6
1 a few days ago
2 get back to me asap, please
3 by tomorrow morning
4 I spoke to your colleague
5 Could you please send
6 as soon as possible

Exercise 7
Emmanuel sends the email high priority (!) and adds the word "Reminder" to the subject line. He also uses words like "urgent", "due tomorrow", and "by the end of the day" to show how urgent the email is.

Exercise 8
1 b 2 d 3 a 4 c

Exercise 9
1 large 2 201614 3 three 4 urgent
5 pay the invoice 6 Karina or Bob

(model answer)
To: John Leach@Baxwell Ltd
From: Karina Meyer
CC: Bob Haslam
Subject: Reminder – invoice # 201614
Dear John,
I am writing about the order you would like to place.
Unfortunately, your last invoice (#201614) was due three weeks ago and is still outstanding. We need to receive payment before we can start working on / processing your order.
Please contact me or Bob if you have any questions.
Best,
Karina

Exercises 10–12 (open answers)

Unit 5
....

Exercise 1 (open answers)

Exercise 2
Graham is asking for the update. Yes, he gets the information he needs.
Finished tasks: get new brochures, put training video online

Exercise 3
No, it is not all good news. The Czech translation of the documentation is not ready yet.

Exercise 4

1 Can you update me on **what's happening with** the new product range?
2 Just a **quick email to update you on** the current status of your order: …
3 We **have received** the customer brochures from head office.
4 Samples **will be here** by next week.
5 We are **ready to deliver** your order – …
6 … it's **currently with** the logistics dept.
7 Unfortunately, we are **behind schedule** with the documentation …
8 I'll contact you again **as soon as** I have more information.
9 I'll speak with the translator and **get back to you** by the end of the week.

Exercise 5

1 I'll contact you as soon as I have more information.
2 The report will be in your inbox by Friday.
3 We've finished the training video.
4 There are still some open questions.
5 This is the current status of the project.
6 We are behind schedule with the brochures.

a beginning: 5
b middle: 2, 3, 4, 6
c end: 1, 2

Exercise 6

1 have/'ve reserved
2 is/'s … organizing
3 will/'ll send
4 have not / haven't finished
5 are/'re … waiting
6 will/'ll give

Exercise 7

No, it is not all bad news. Andrea can do the training.
The two mistakes in the notes are:
- problems with ~~our~~ Skywise's system
- Andrea can do ~~documentation~~ training

Exercise 8

(model answer)
No, he doesn't only describe the problems. He also makes suggestions to solve the problems and offers to discuss details over the phone.

Exercise 9

1 This is **due to an emergency** that my team had to work on.
2 We don't have an installation date from you yet, **so it's difficult** to plan my technicians.
3 I have asked Andrea to train your staff **because** your team already knows her.
4 We could **either put more staff** on the project …
5 … **or install** the system at a later date.
6 If it is still not working, **maybe we could** help you with it.
7 **How about having** a video call soon to discuss the details?

Exercise 10

1 due to
2 but
3 Either, or
4 so
5 because
6 so

Exercises 11–13 (open answers)

Unit 6

Exercise 1 (open answers)

Exercise 2

who:	Matthias Brand	Anton Feistinger
when:	next Thursday at 6 p.m.	Tuesday, November 5
where:	Park Hotel restaurant	his company/office
why:	to discuss new project	to present new product range

Email 1: Sally seems to know Matthias well. She uses his first name and she writes about a project they are working on together. Perhaps they are colleagues or close business partners.

Email 2: Lionel and Mr. Feistinger are new business contacts. They met recently at a trade fair and haven't done business together yet.

Exercise 3

1 Matthias accepts the invitation.
2 He doesn't like the restaurant at the Park Hotel.
3 Mr. Feistinger can't meet because he will be on a business trip / away.

Exercise 4

1 Would you **have time to meet for** dinner?
2 Let me know if that would **work for** you.
3 We … would like to **meet to present** our new product range …
4 Would Thursday evening at 6:00 p.m. **be OK for you**?
5 We … could come to your office at whatever time **is convenient for you**.
6 … but **how about meeting** at a different restaurant?
7 Thursday's **good for** me …
8 I'm afraid a meeting on the day you suggest **isn't possible** because …

Exercise 5

1 Do you have time to meet for lunch tomorrow?
2 Can we meet on Monday? I'm free in the afternoon.
3 Would Friday morning at 9:00 be convenient?
4 How about meeting at the reception desk?
5 I'm free on Tuesday afternoon.

1 c 2 a 3 e 4 d 5 b

Exercise 6

1 in 2 at 3 on 4 from 5 on 6 at

Exercise 7

1 Could we *(remember, capital letter!)*
2 like to
3 Unfortunately
4 How about
5 work for you
6 fine for me
7 See you

Exercise 8

Christof needs to change his plans because he has to go to a client's (office).
Silke says that "something has come up at short notice" and that's why she needs to change her plans. She doesn't give any details.

Exercise 9

1 I'm afraid **I have to cancel** our meeting tomorrow.
2 Can we meet on Thursday at around 3 p.m. **instead**?
3 Unfortunately, something has come up **at short notice** …
4 Would it be possible to **move the meeting** to four o'clock?
5 Sorry for **the inconvenience**.

Exercise 10

1 Miguel asks Amy to go on a business trip to Geneva.
2 Amy has a meeting planned with Mark Jones from Great Foods.
3 She will write an email to Mark Jones to cancel the meeting and suggest another date.

(model answer)
Dear Mark
Unfortunately, a trip to Geneva has come up at short notice and I have to cancel our meeting on Tuesday. Would it be possible to meet on Monday, November 8 at the same time instead?
Sorry for the inconvenience.
Regards
Amanda

Exercises 11 + 12 (open answers)

Unit 7 ....

Exercise 1 (open answers)

Exercise 2
clarify information: 1, 4
ask for confirmation: 2, 3

Emails – subject lines
a 3 b 2 c 1 d 4

(model answer)
The subject lines of b and d are clear and effective.
Suggestions for a and c:
a Subject: Travel details Mr. Lee, July 5-8
c Subject: Questions about minutes

Exercise 3

1 I'm writing the minutes … and there are a few points **I'm not sure about**.
2 … Below is a **summary of** our telephone conversation.
3 I need to **make sure I have** all of Mr. Lee's travel details.
4 **Just wanted to clarify** what we spoke about yesterday …
5 Can you please **check the following**?
6 The report is due on Tuesday. (Or **was that** Thursday?)
7 We will change the deadline to Sept. 1. (Is that **what we agreed**?)
8 **Does that mean** that no one will be in Accounting that day?
9 Please let me know if anything's **incorrect or missing**.
10 Can you please **confirm the above**?

Exercise 4

1 summary 2 points 3 sure 4 check 5 get back
6 agreed 7 mean 8 was that

Exercise 5
(model answers)

1 Did you mean in-house at our company or your company.
2 Was that $13 or $30?
3 Do you mean the plant in Poland or the one in Ukraine?
4 Did you mean (send it) as a PDF in an email or by mail?
5 Was that the 10th or 17th?

Exercise 6

Ellen corrects the day Johanna should contact Mr. Novak (Monday, not Friday). She suggests that they meet at the airport and not in the office.

Exercise 7

1 Thank you **for the summary of** our discussion.
2 It looks good, but I have **a few changes**.
3 I've **added my comments** to your email below.
4 **Actually**, could we meet at the airport instead?
5 It's fine, **but** contact him on Monday.

Exercise 8

1 I've added my comments to your email.
2 Thank you for the notes from our meeting.
3 It looks good, but I've found a few mistakes. See notes in red below.
4 It's fine, but the price is €13 (not 30).
5 Actually, we agreed to deliver by June 16, not July.
6 I just wanted to confirm that everything's correct.

Exercise 9
(model answers)
Pierre needs to clarify when they are moving offices, when the staff needs to work from home and when they can start working in the new building.
Yes, he has answers to all of his questions.
Silvia offers to answer Pierre's questions in writing to make sure there is no misunderstanding *(Missverständnis)*.

Exercise 10
(model answer)

Hi Pierre

Thanks for your email. There are a few points to correct.
First of all, you are right: the move is on Friday,
August 22.
The staff can work from home on Friday but they need to
be back in the office on Monday.
The IT systems will be in operation by Monday morning
(not Tuesday morning).
Let me know if you have any more questions.
Regards
Silvia

Exercises 11 + 12 (open answers)

Unit 8

Exercise 1
(open answers)

Exercise 2
a 3 a printing mistake
b 1 a late shipment
c 2 the wrong information

Exercise 3
1 We are writing **to complain about a delay** with our order.
2 I am afraid you sent me the **wrong figures** yesterday.
3 This is to let you know that **we are disappointed** with the brochures …
4 Please **let me know** when the order will arrive.
5 Can you please **look into the matter** …
6 … and suggest **a solution**?

Exercise 4
1 disappointed   2 short notice
3 look into   4 contact
5 complain   6 satisfied
7 lower   8 proceed

Exercise 5
(model answer)

Dear Milan

I am writing to complain about the organization for the
training day. It begins tomorrow afternoon and we haven't
received the manuals yet. Could you please let me know
when you sent them / when they will arrive?
Please look into the matter and tell me how we should
proceed.
Best

Exercise 6 (open answer)

Exercise 7
1 We **apologize for** the delay in delivery.
2 **Sorry about** sending the wrong document.
3 Please **accept our apologies** for the mistake.
4 We **will replace** the cards right away.
5 As a **gesture of goodwill**, …
6 … this order will be **free of charge**, and …
7 … we would also like to **offer you a discount** of 10% on your next order.
8 We hope this solution is **satisfactory for you**.

Exercise 8
1 d Please accept our apologies for cancelling the installation date at such short notice.
2 a This was due to illness and we are looking into the matter.
3 e I have looked at the schedule and we can install the system next Monday.
4 c Please let me know if that is convenient for you.
5 f As a gesture of goodwill, we would also like to offer you a 10% discount on the installation service.
6 b We hope you are satisfied with this solution.

Exercise 9
1 overcharged Techtoys
2 €8,530
3 has already paid
4 the change to a new accounting system
5 refund the difference
6 five

(model answer)

Dear Stella,

We apologize for overcharging you / the wrong price on
the invoice / the mistake on the invoice. We will refund
the difference and would also like to offer you a 5%
discount on your next order.
We hope you are satisfied with this solution.
Sorry again for the mistake.
Best regards,
Axel

Exercises 10–12 (open answers)

Model emails

Out of office reply

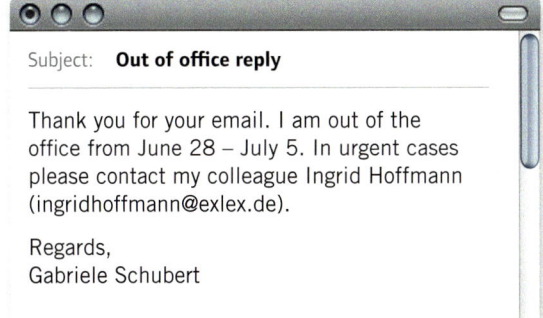

Subject: Out of office reply

Thank you for your email. I am out of the office from June 28 – July 5. In urgent cases please contact my colleague Ingrid Hoffmann (ingridhoffmann@exlex.de).

Regards,
Gabriele Schubert

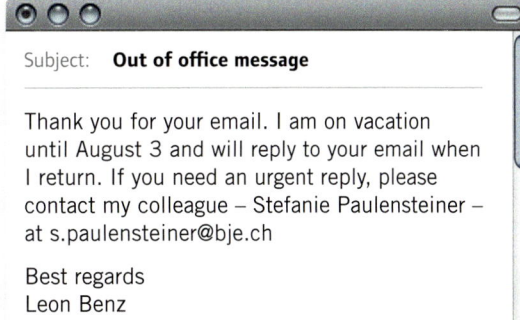

Subject: Out of office message

Thank you for your email. I am on vacation until August 3 and will reply to your email when I return. If you need an urgent reply, please contact my colleague – Stefanie Paulensteiner – at s.paulensteiner@bje.ch

Best regards
Leon Benz

Asking for information

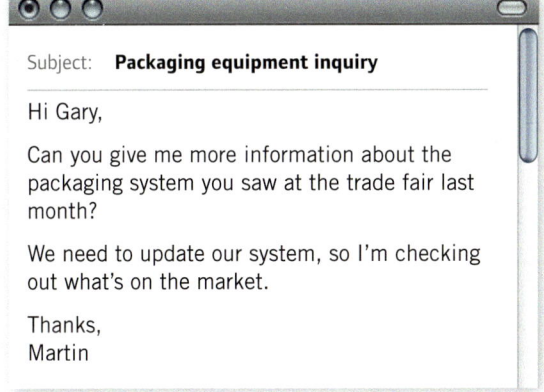

Subject: Packaging equipment inquiry

Hi Gary,

Can you give me more information about the packaging system you saw at the trade fair last month?

We need to update our system, so I'm checking out what's on the market.

Thanks,
Martin

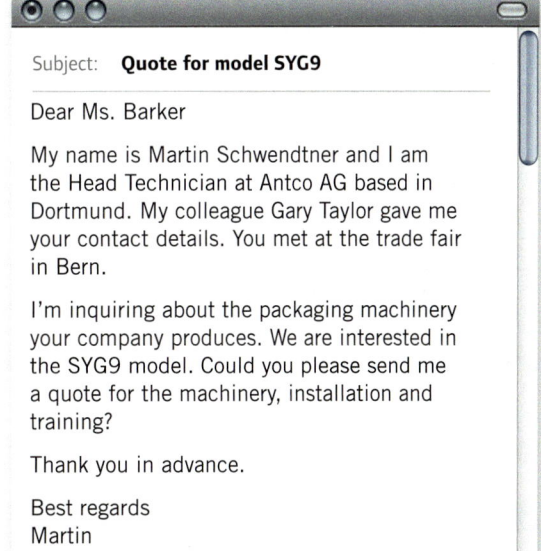

Subject: Quote for model SYG9

Dear Ms. Barker

My name is Martin Schwendtner and I am the Head Technician at Antco AG based in Dortmund. My colleague Gary Taylor gave me your contact details. You met at the trade fair in Bern.

I'm inquiring about the packaging machinery your company produces. We are interested in the SYG9 model. Could you please send me a quote for the machinery, installation and training?

Thank you in advance.

Best regards
Martin

Giving information

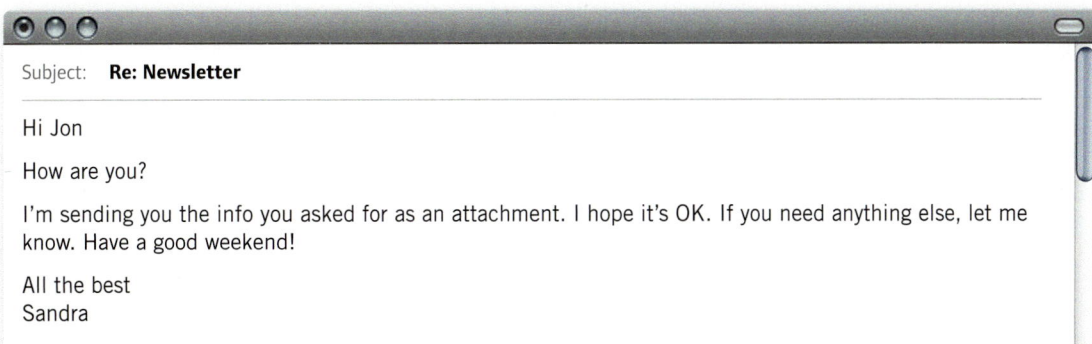

Subject: Re: Newsletter

Hi Jon

How are you?

I'm sending you the info you asked for as an attachment. I hope it's OK. If you need anything else, let me know. Have a good weekend!

All the best
Sandra

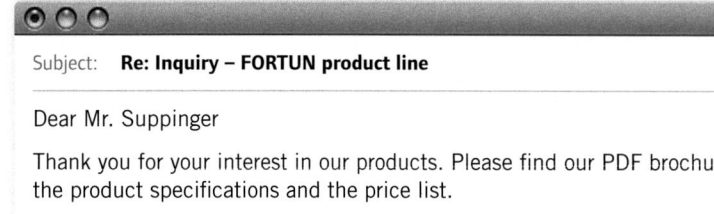

Subject: **Re: Inquiry – FORTUN product line**

Dear Mr. Suppinger

Thank you for your interest in our products. Please find our PDF brochure in the attachment. It contains all the product specifications and the price list.

Please contact me if you have further questions. We would be happy to arrange a meeting to discuss your requirements.

Regards
Nigel Johnston

Requesting action

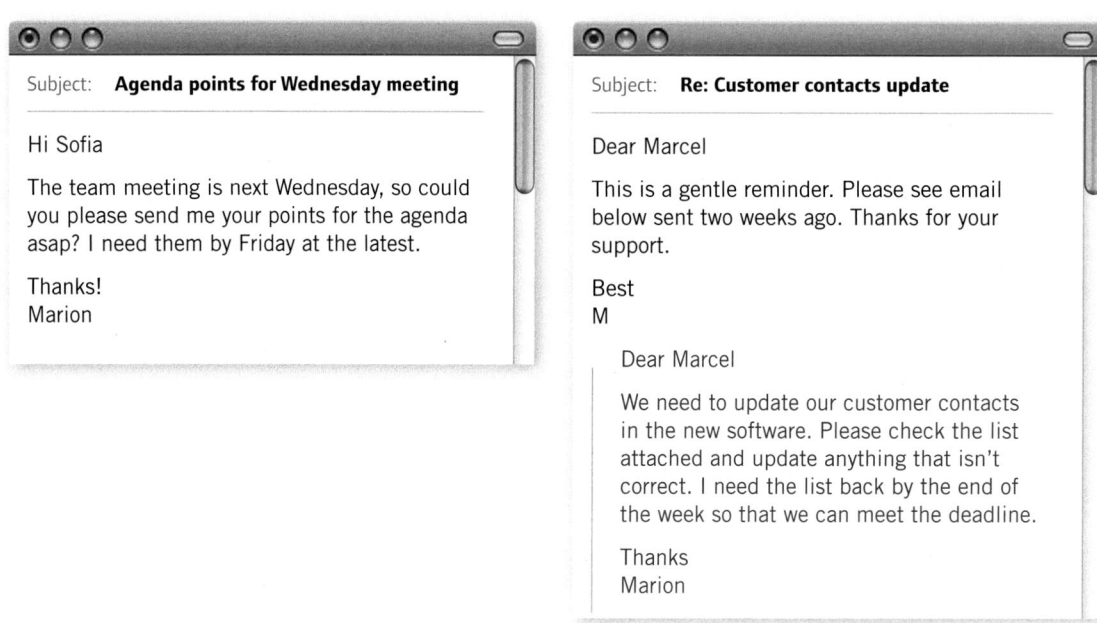

Subject: **Agenda points for Wednesday meeting**

Hi Sofia

The team meeting is next Wednesday, so could you please send me your points for the agenda asap? I need them by Friday at the latest.

Thanks!
Marion

Subject: **Re: Customer contacts update**

Dear Marcel

This is a gentle reminder. Please see email below sent two weeks ago. Thanks for your support.

Best
M

> Dear Marcel
>
> We need to update our customer contacts in the new software. Please check the list attached and update anything that isn't correct. I need the list back by the end of the week so that we can meet the deadline.
>
> Thanks
> Marion

Requesting urgent action

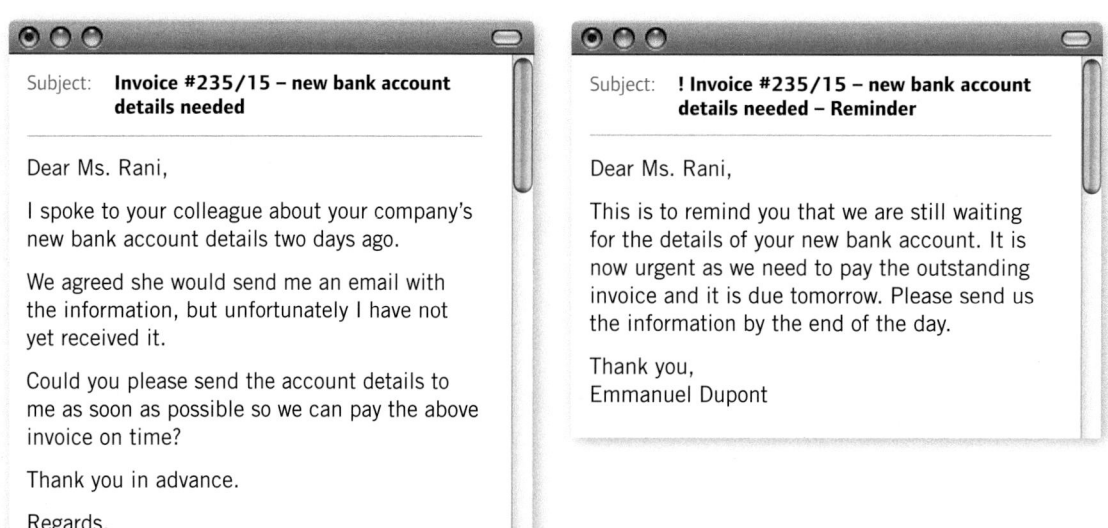

Subject: **Invoice #235/15 – new bank account details needed**

Dear Ms. Rani,

I spoke to your colleague about your company's new bank account details two days ago.

We agreed she would send me an email with the information, but unfortunately I have not yet received it.

Could you please send the account details to me as soon as possible so we can pay the above invoice on time?

Thank you in advance.

Regards,
Emmanuel Dupont

Subject: **! Invoice #235/15 – new bank account details needed – Reminder**

Dear Ms. Rani,

This is to remind you that we are still waiting for the details of your new bank account. It is now urgent as we need to pay the outstanding invoice and it is due tomorrow. Please send us the information by the end of the day.

Thank you,
Emmanuel Dupont

Asking for an update

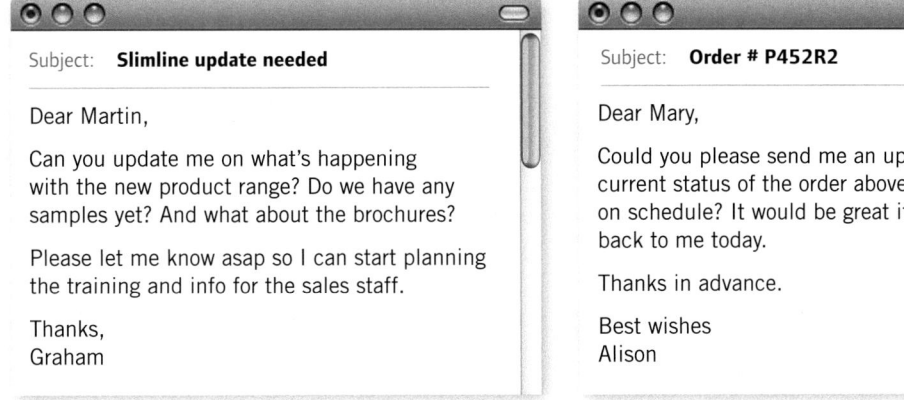

Subject: **Slimline update needed**

Dear Martin,

Can you update me on what's happening with the new product range? Do we have any samples yet? And what about the brochures?

Please let me know asap so I can start planning the training and info for the sales staff.

Thanks,
Graham

Subject: **Order # P452R2**

Dear Mary,

Could you please send me an update on the current status of the order above? Is everything on schedule? It would be great if you could get back to me today.

Thanks in advance.

Best wishes
Alison

Giving updates

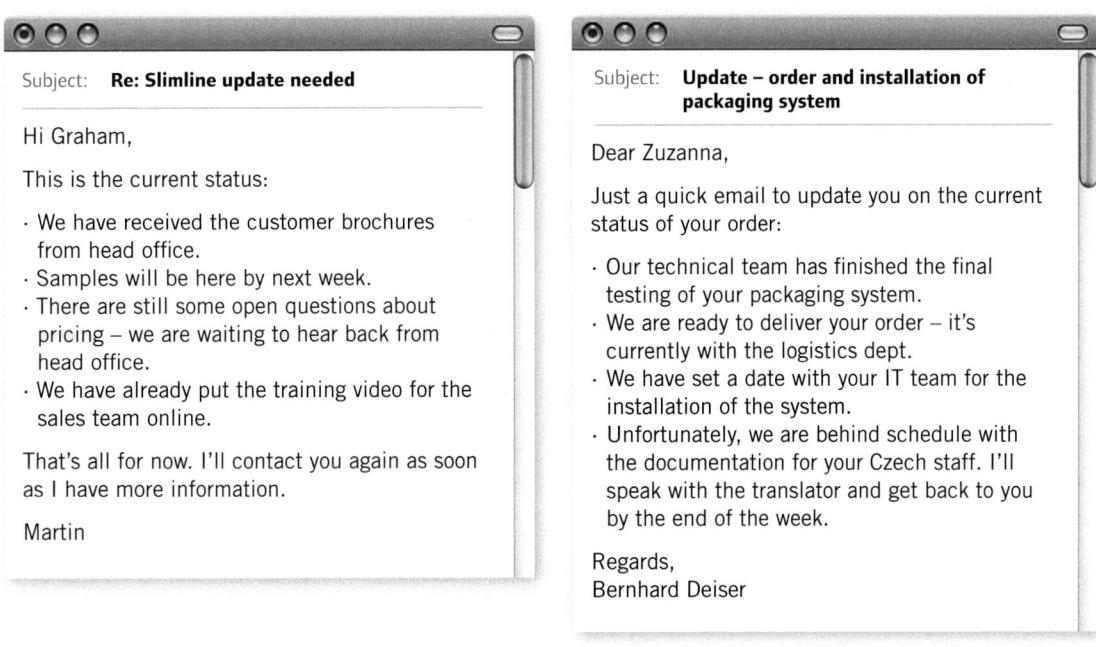

Subject: **Re: Slimline update needed**

Hi Graham,

This is the current status:

· We have received the customer brochures from head office.
· Samples will be here by next week.
· There are still some open questions about pricing – we are waiting to hear back from head office.
· We have already put the training video for the sales team online.

That's all for now. I'll contact you again as soon as I have more information.

Martin

Subject: **Update – order and installation of packaging system**

Dear Zuzanna,

Just a quick email to update you on the current status of your order:

· Our technical team has finished the final testing of your packaging system.
· We are ready to deliver your order – it's currently with the logistics dept.
· We have set a date with your IT team for the installation of the system.
· Unfortunately, we are behind schedule with the documentation for your Czech staff. I'll speak with the translator and get back to you by the end of the week.

Regards,
Bernhard Deiser

Making arrangements

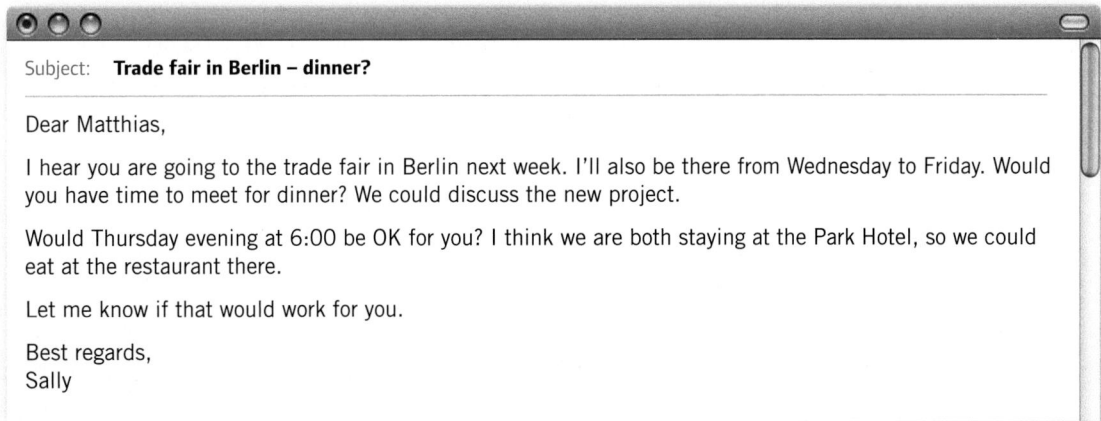

Subject: **Trade fair in Berlin – dinner?**

Dear Matthias,

I hear you are going to the trade fair in Berlin next week. I'll also be there from Wednesday to Friday. Would you have time to meet for dinner? We could discuss the new project.

Would Thursday evening at 6:00 be OK for you? I think we are both staying at the Park Hotel, so we could eat at the restaurant there.

Let me know if that would work for you.

Best regards,
Sally

Subject: **Meeting re new product range**

Dear Mr. Feistinger

It was nice meeting you at the trade fair.

We will be in Leipzig at the beginning of November and would like to meet to present our new product range to you and your team.

We are free on Tuesday, November 5, and could come to your office at whatever time is convenient for you.

I look forward to your reply.

Best wishes
Lionel Pellegrini

Changing appointments

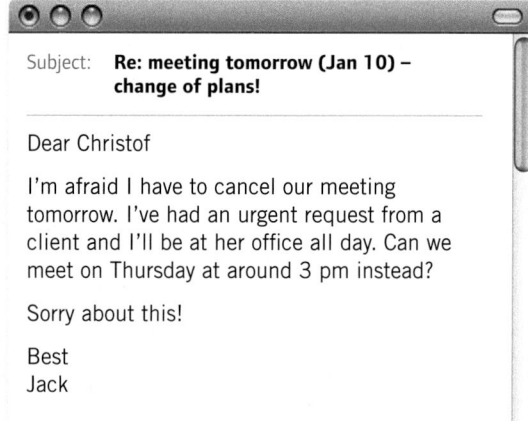

Subject: **Re: meeting tomorrow (Jan 10) – change of plans!**

Dear Christof

I'm afraid I have to cancel our meeting tomorrow. I've had an urgent request from a client and I'll be at her office all day. Can we meet on Thursday at around 3 pm instead?

Sorry about this!

Best
Jack

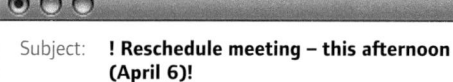

Subject: **! Reschedule meeting – this afternoon (April 6)!**

Dear Mrs. Grimani,

I'm writing about our meeting this afternoon. Unfortunately, something has come up at short notice so I won't be able to meet at 2:30. Would it be possible to move the meeting to four o'clock?

Sorry for the inconvenience.

Best wishes,
Silke Liebig

Checking information

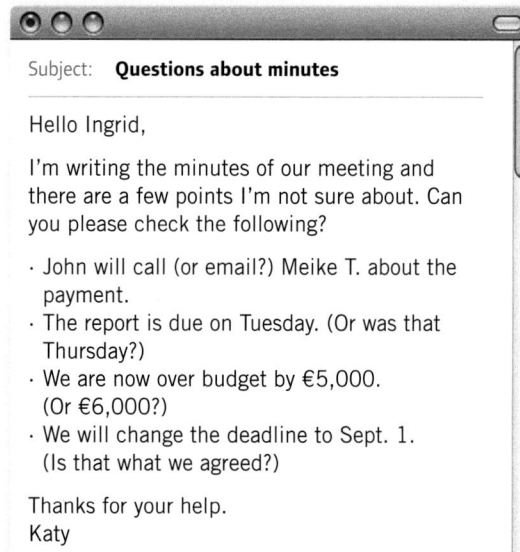

Subject: **Questions about minutes**

Hello Ingrid,

I'm writing the minutes of our meeting and there are a few points I'm not sure about. Can you please check the following?

· John will call (or email?) Meike T. about the payment.
· The report is due on Tuesday. (Or was that Thursday?)
· We are now over budget by €5,000. (Or €6,000?)
· We will change the deadline to Sept. 1. (Is that what we agreed?)

Thanks for your help.
Katy

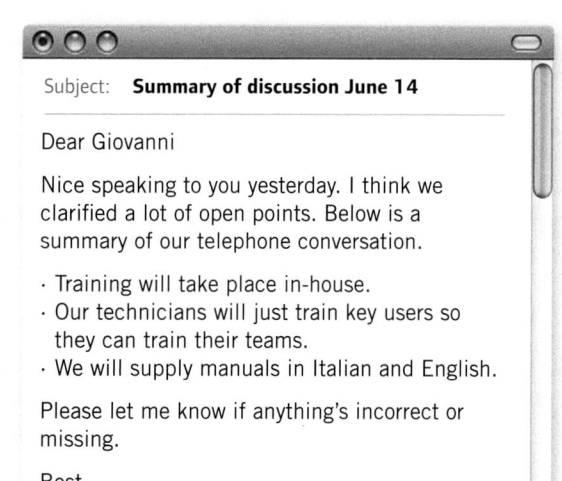

Subject: **Summary of discussion June 14**

Dear Giovanni

Nice speaking to you yesterday. I think we clarified a lot of open points. Below is a summary of our telephone conversation.

· Training will take place in-house.
· Our technicians will just train key users so they can train their teams.
· We will supply manuals in Italian and English.

Please let me know if anything's incorrect or missing.

Best
Manuel

Making a complaint

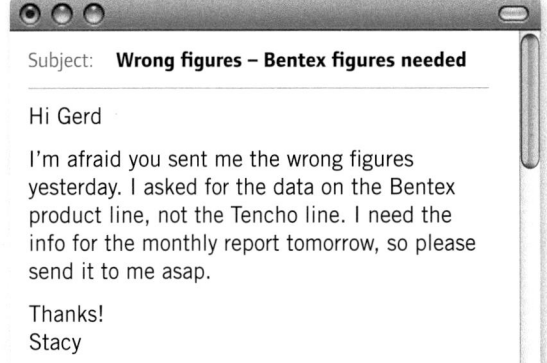

Subject: **Wrong figures – Bentex figures needed**

Hi Gerd

I'm afraid you sent me the wrong figures yesterday. I asked for the data on the Bentex product line, not the Tencho line. I need the info for the monthly report tomorrow, so please send it to me asap.

Thanks!
Stacy

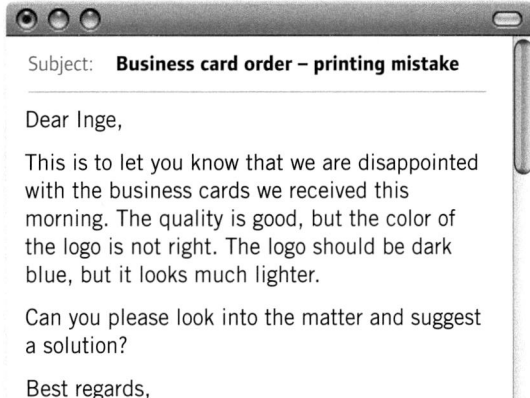

Subject: **Business card order – printing mistake**

Dear Inge,

This is to let you know that we are disappointed with the business cards we received this morning. The quality is good, but the color of the logo is not right. The logo should be dark blue, but it looks much lighter.

Can you please look into the matter and suggest a solution?

Best regards,
Patricia

Replying to a complaint

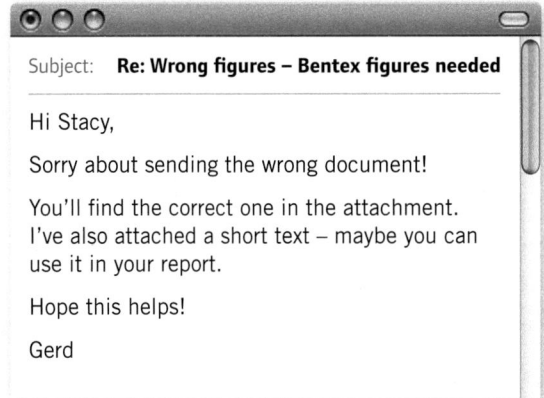

Subject: **Re: Wrong figures – Bentex figures needed**

Hi Stacy,

Sorry about sending the wrong document!

You'll find the correct one in the attachment. I've also attached a short text – maybe you can use it in your report.

Hope this helps!

Gerd

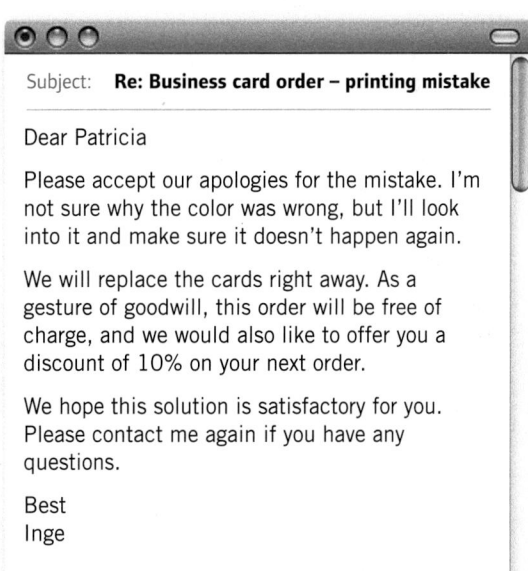

Subject: **Re: Business card order – printing mistake**

Dear Patricia

Please accept our apologies for the mistake. I'm not sure why the color was wrong, but I'll look into it and make sure it doesn't happen again.

We will replace the cards right away. As a gesture of goodwill, this order will be free of charge, and we would also like to offer you a discount of 10% on your next order.

We hope this solution is satisfactory for you. Please contact me again if you have any questions.

Best
Inge

Key phrases

Greetings	Begrüßungen
Dear *(first name)*	Liebe/r *(Vorname),*
Dear Mr./Mrs./Ms. *(last name)*	Sehr geehrte/r Herr/Frau *(Nachname),*
Dear Sir or Madam	Sehr geehrte Damen und Herren,
Dear all	Liebe alle,
Dear Sam and Gina	Lieber Sam, liebe Gina,
Hi/Hello *(first name)*	Hi/Hallo *(Vorname),*

Starting an email	Eine E-Mail beginnen
Thank you for your email.	Danke für Ihre E-Mail.
It was nice speaking to / seeing you just now.	Es war schön, mit Ihnen zu sprechen / Sie zu treffen.
I am writing about/concerning …	Ich schreibe bezüglich/betreffend …
I'm writing to ask/inquire about …	Ich schreibe, um nach … zu fragen.
I am contacting you about …	Ich kontaktiere Sie betreffend …
Concerning the meeting / your question, …	Bezüglich des Meetings / Ihrer Frage, …
Please find … attached.	Ich habe … angefügt.
I am forwarding your email to …	Ich leite Ihre Mail weiter an …

Closing an email	Eine E-Mail beenden
I hope you had a good vacation.	Ich hoffe, dass Sie einen angenehmen Urlaub hatten.
Thanks.	Danke.
I look forward to hearing from you.	Ich freue mich darauf, von Ihnen zu hören.
Looking forward to your reply.	Ich freue mich auf Ihre Antwort.

Closes	Briefschlüsse
Best regards · Best wishes	Beste Grüße, · Viele Grüße,
Regards · Best · All the best	Gruß, · Schönen Gruß · Schöne Grüße,
Thanks	Danke

What to do with an email: you can …	Wie eine E-Mail versenden: Sie können …
send it	sie verschicken
send it high priority	sie mit hoher Priorität verschicken
as an urgent message	sie als dringende Nachricht schicken
receive it	sie erhalten
reply to / answer it	sie beantworten
forward it to somebody	sie an jemanden weiterleiten
attach a document to it	ein Dokument anfügen
print it	sie ausdrucken

Asking for information (neutral)	**Um Information bitten (neutral)**
Could you please send me …?	Könnten Sie mir bitte … schicken?
Could you please let me know about …?	Könnten Sie mir bitte wegen … Bescheid geben?
I'd like some information about the …	Ich hätte gerne einige Informationen zu …
I/We need (to) …	Ich/Wir brauchen (müssen) …
Can/Could you (please) send it as an attachment to me?	Können/Könnten Sie es mir (bitte) als Anhang schicken?

Asking for information (more formal)	**Um Informationen bitten (formeller)**
I am writing to request some information about …	Ich schreibe Ihnen, da ich gerne ein paar Informationen zu … hätte.
I am contacting you because …	Ich schreibe Ihnen wegen …
I'm inquiring about the …	Ich möchte mich wegen … erkundigen.
We are interested in the new model / in purchasing …	Wir sind an dem neuen Modell interessiert / daran interessiert, … zu kaufen.
Could you (please) send me/us a quotation/ quote for …?	Können Sie mir/uns (bitte) ein Angebot / einen Preis für … schicken?

Introducing yourself	**Sich vorstellen**
My name is …	Mein Name ist …
I am the Head Technician / a buyer at *(company name)*.	Ich bin der leitende Techniker / Einkäufer bei *(Firmenname)*.
I work in the marketing department at *(company name)*.	Ich arbeite in der Marketingabteilung bei *(Firmenname)*.
I work for (company name) based in *(city)*.	Ich arbeite bei *(Firmenname)* in *(Stadt)*.
I received your name from my/your colleague in the … department.	Ich habe Ihren Namen von meinem/Ihren Kollegen aus der … Abteilung erhalten.
My/Your colleague in the … department / … office gave me your contact details.	Mein/Ihr Kollege aus der … Abteilung / dem … Büro hat mir Ihre Kontaktdaten gegeben.

Departments	**Abteilungen**
accounting	Buchhaltung
customer service	Kundenbetreuung
finance	Finanzabteilung
HR (human resources)	Personalabteilung
IT (information technology)	IT
marketing	Marketing
production	Herstellung
purchasing	Einkauf
R&D (research and development)	F&E (Forschung und Entwicklung)
sales	Vertrieb, Verkauf

Closing a request	**Eine Anfrage abschließen**
Thanks. / Thank you.	Danke. / Vielen Dank.
Thank you in advance.	Vielen Dank im Voraus.

Opening sentences (to someone you know)	**Einleitungssätze (an jemand Bekanntes)**
How are you?	Wie geht es Ihnen?
I hope you're well.	Ich hoffe, es geht Ihnen gut.
It's nice to hear from you again.	Es ist schön, von Ihnen zu hören.
Beginning a reply	**Eine Antwort beginnen**
Thank you for contacting me/us about …	Danke für Ihre Anfrage bezüglich …
Regarding your request, …	Hinsichtlich Ihrer Anfrage, …
Regarding the information you need, …	Hinsichtlich der Information, die Sie benötigen, …
Thank you for your interest in our product(s).	Danke für Ihr Interesse an unserem Produkt / unseren Produkten.
Sending information	**Informationen verschicken**
I've attached … / I'm attaching …	Ich habe … angefügt.
Please find the … attached.	Angefügt finden Sie …
I'm sending you the info(rmation) you asked for as an / in the attachment.	Die von Ihnen erbetenen Informationen finden Sie im Anhang.
You can / Please use the link below to …	Bitte nutzen Sie den unten stehenden Link, um zu …
Offering further help	**Weitere Hilfe anbieten**
Please contact me if you have further questions / need (any) more help.	Bitte setzen Sie sich mit mir in Verbindung, falls Sie noch weitere Fragen haben / weitere Hilfe benötigen.
Feel free to contact me if you need anything else.	Sagen Sie gerne Bescheid, wenn Sie noch etwas benötigen.
I'd be glad to give you a demonstration / send you more information.	Gerne werde ich es Ihnen einmal zeigen / Ihnen mehr Informationen zukommen lassen.
We would be happy to arrange a meeting to discuss your requirements.	Gerne vereinbaren wir ein Treffen mit Ihnen, um über Ihren Bedarf zu sprechen.
Closing sentences (to someone you know)	**Briefabschlüsse (an jemand Bekanntes)**
See you at the meeting next week.	Bis nächste Woche beim Meeting.
Have a good weekend.	Ich wünsche Ihnen ein schönes Wochenende.

Explaining the situation

This is to let you know that invoice no. … is outstanding.

I am writing to let you know that …

I am writing about/concerning/regarding …

This is a gentle reminder.

I spoke to your colleague … two days ago.

Die Situation erklären

Hiermit möchten wir Sie darauf hinweisen, dass die Rechnung Nr. … noch aussteht.

Ich schreibe, um Ihnen mitzuteilen, dass …

Ich schreibe wegen/bezüglich …

Ich möchte Sie noch einmal freundlich daran erinnern.

Ich habe vor zwei Tagen mit Ihrem Kollegen … gesprochen.

Requesting action

Please transfer the payment / check the list / send me …

Could you please send …?

Um Handlung bitten

Bitte überweisen Sie das Geld / überprüfen Sie die Liste / schicken Sie mir …

Können Sie bitte … schicken?

Giving a deadline

Please get back to me by April 30.

I need the information by Friday at the latest.

I need the list back by the end of the week.

The list needs to be on my desk by/on Thursday.

The payment/report is due tomorrow.

Eine Frist setzen

Bitte sagen Sie mir bis zum 30. April Bescheid.

Ich brauche die Information bis spätestens Freitag.

Ich brauche die Liste bis zum Ende der Woche wieder zurück.

Die Liste muss bis (Donnerstag) wieder bei mir sein.

Die Zahlung / Der Bericht ist morgen fällig.

Saying something is urgent

Please get back to me / contact me as soon as possible so that we can …

Please reply/answer as soon as you can.

It is important that we receive your decision / the report by the end of the day/week.

Unfortunately, … is urgent as we need to …

Could/Can you please send it right away?

Sagen, dass etwas dringlich ist

Bitte melden Sie sich bei mir / kontaktieren Sie mich so bald wie möglich, damit wir …

Bitte antworten Sie so bald wie möglich.

Es ist wichtig, dass wir Ihre Entscheidung / den Bericht bis zum Ende des Tages / der Woche erhalten.

Leider ist … sehr dringend, da wir … müssen.

Könnten/Können Sie es bitte sofort schicken?

Asking for an update	Eine Update einfordern
Can you update me on what's happening with …?	Können Sie mir ein Update über … geben?
Can you tell me the current status of …?	Können Sie mir den aktuellen Status von … mitteilen?

Starting an update	Ein Update beginnen
Just a quick email to update you on the …	Dies ist nur eine kurze Mail, um Ihnen ein Update über … zu geben.
This is the situation at the moment: …	Das ist die derzeitige Situation: …
This is the current status: …	Das ist der aktuelle Status: …
Here's an update on …	Hier ist ein Update …

Giving an update	Ein Update geben
We have set a date with …	Wir haben einen Termin mit … abgemacht.
Our team has finished …	Unser Team hat … fertig gestellt / erledigt.
Unfortunately, we haven't finished … yet.	Leider haben wir … noch nicht fertig gestellt / erledigt.
We are behind schedule with …	Wir liegen mit … hinter dem Zeitplan.
We are ready to …	Wir sind bereit, um …
I am currently organizing …	Zurzeit organisiere ich …
We are waiting to hear back from …	Wir warten darauf, von … zu hören.
Samples will be here by next week.	Proben werden bis zur nächsten Woche hier sein.
I will send the information tomorrow.	Ich werde die Informationen morgen schicken.

Giving reasons	Gründe angeben
This is due to …	Das liegt an …
I have … because …	Ich habe …, da …
We don't have …, so it's difficult to …	Wir haben kein/e …, deshalb ist es schwierig zu …

Making suggestions	Vorschläge machen
We could either … or …	Wir könnten entweder … oder …
If it is still not working, maybe we could …	Falls es noch immer nicht funktioniert, vielleicht könnten wir …
How about having …?	Wie wäre es mit …?
Should I …?	

Ending an update	Ein Update abschließen
That's all for now.	Das ist fürs Erste alles.
I'll contact you again as soon as I have more information.	Ich melde mich, sobald ich mehr Informationen habe.
I'll get back to you by the end of the week.	Ich melde mich bei Ihnen bis zum Ende der Woche.

Arranging an appointment

Would you have time to meet for dinner?

We would like to meet to discuss …

How about meeting on Tuesday?

Let me know if that would work for you.

Einen Termin vereinbaren

Hätten Sie Zeit, sich zum Abendessen zu treffen?

Wir würde uns gerne treffen, um über … zu sprechen.

Wie wäre es mit einem Treffen am Donnerstag?

Sagen Sie Bescheid, ob das für Sie in Ordnung geht.

Suggesting a time and place

Would Thursday evening at 6:00 be OK/good for you?

Would Friday morning be convenient?

Could we meet on Wednesday at 10:00 a.m.?

We could come to your office at whatever time is convenient for you.

How about meeting at/on …?

Zeit und Ort vorschlagen

Ist Donnerstabend 6:00 Uhr für Sie OK?

Würde Ihnen Freitagmorgen passen?

Können wir uns am Mittwoch um 10 Uhr treffen?

Wir können zu Ihrem Büro kommen, wann immer es Ihnen am besten passt.

Wie wäre es mit einem Treffen am/um …?

Accepting an invitation

It's a good idea to meet next week.

Wednesday is good/fine for me.

Three o'clock would work for me.

See you on Monday.

See you then.

Eine Einladung annehmen

Es ist eine gute Idee, sich nächste Woche zu treffen.

Mittwoch passt mir gut.

Drei Uhr würde gehen.

Bis Montag.

Wir sehen uns bald.

Declining an invitation

I'm afraid a meeting on the day you suggest is not possible.

Unfortunately, I won't be in the office on …

Sorry, Tuesday won't work for me.

Eine Einladung ablehnen

Leider können wir uns an dem von Ihnen vorgeschlagenen Tag nicht treffen.

Am … werde ich leider nicht im Büro sein.

Tut mir leid, aber Dienstag passt bei mir nicht.

Changing an appointment

I'm afraid I have to cancel our meeting tomorrow.

Unfortunately, something has come up at short notice.

Can we meet on Thursday at around 3:00 p.m. instead?

Would it be possible to move the meeting to four o'clock?

Sorry about this.

Sorry for the inconvenience.

Einen Termin verlegen

Ich muss unseren Termin morgen leider absagen.

Leider ist kurzfristig etwas dazwischen gekommen.

Können wir uns stattdessen am Donnerstag um 15:00 Uhr treffen?

Ist es möglich, das Meeting auf vier Uhr zu verschieben?

Es tut mir leid.

Bitte entschuldigen Sie die Unannehmlichkeiten.

Starting the email

I'm writing the minutes ... and there are a few points I'm not sure about.

Below is a summary of our telephone conversation.

Here is a summary of our discussion ...

Just wanted to clarify what we spoke about yesterday ...

I need to make sure I have ... . See below: ...

Eine E-Mail beginnen

Ich schreibe gerade das Protokoll und habe einige Punkte, bei denen ich mir nicht ganz sicher bin.

Weiter unten finden Sie eine Zusammenfassung unseres Telefongesprächs.

Hier ist eine Zusammenfassung unserer Diskussion.

Ich wollte nur noch mal in Bezug auf das gestrige Thema Klarheit schaffen ...

Ich muss sicherstellen, dass ich ... habe. Siehe unten: ...

Checking and clarifying information

Can you please check the following?

Can you check the details below?

Or was that ...?

Or did you mean ...?

Is that what we agreed?

Is that right?

Does that mean that ...?

Informationen überprüfen und klären

Können Sie bitte Folgendes überprüfen?

Können Sie bitte die Einzelheiten weiter unten überprüfen?

Oder war das ...?

Oder meinten Sie ...?

Hatten wir uns darauf geeinigt?

Stimmt das?

Bedeutet das, dass ...?

Asking for confirmation

Please let me know if anything's incorrect or missing.

Can you please confirm the above / the following?

Um Bestätigung bitten

Bitte lassen Sie mich wissen, falls irgendwas unzutreffend ist oder fehlt.

Können Sie bitte Obiges / das Folgende bestätigen?

Correcting and confirming information

Thank you for the summary of our discussion.

It looks good, but I have a few changes.

Thank you for the notes from our meeting.

I've just found a few mistakes.

I've added my comments to your email below.

Actually, ...

It's fine, but ...

I've read your summary and can confirm that everything is correct.

Informationen korrigieren und bestätigen

Danke für die Zusammenfassung unserer Diskussion.

Es sieht gut aus, aber ich habe noch ein paar Änderungen.

Danke für die Notizen zu unserem Meeting.

Ich habe noch ein paar Fehler gefunden.

Ich habe meine Kommentare in Ihrer Mail weiter unten hinzugefügt.

Eigentlich ...

Es ist gut, aber ...

Ich habe Ihre Zusammenfassung gelesen und kann bestätigen, dass alles so stimmt.

Making a complaint | Sich beschweren

I am writing to complain about …	Ich schreibe, um mich wegen … zu beschweren.
This is to let you know that we are disappointed with …	Hiermit möchte ich Sie darüber informieren, dass wir von … enttäuscht sind.
I'm afraid you sent me the wrong figures.	Sie haben mir leider die falschen Zahlen geschickt.
We are not satisfied with the quality.	Wir sind mit der Qualität nicht zufrieden.
We have not received … yet.	Wir haben … bisher nicht erhalten.
The delay is a problem for us, as …	Die Verzögerung stellt für uns ein Problem dar, da …
It should be …, but it is …	Es sollte … sein, aber es ist …

Asking for action | Um Maßnahmen bitte

Please let me know …	Bitte lassen Sie mich wissen, …
Can you please tell me how we should proceed?	Können Sie mich bitte wissen lassen, wie wir weiter vorgehen sollen?
Can you please look into the matter and suggest a solution?	Können Sie bitte der Sache nachgehen und einen Lösungsvorschlag machen?
Please send it to me asap.	Bitte schicken Sie es mir sobald wie möglich.

Apologizing | Sich entschuldigen

We apologize for the delay in delivery.	Wir entschuldigen uns für die Lieferungsverzögerung.
We apologize for the inconvenience.	Wir entschuldigen uns für die Unannehmlichkeiten.
Please accept our apologies for the mistake.	Bitte entschuldigen Sie den Fehler.
Sorry about sending the wrong document.	Es tut mir leid, dass ich das falsche Dokument geschickt habe.
Unfortunately, …	Leider …
I'll look into it and make sure it doesn't happen again.	Ich werde das überprüfen und sicherstellen, dass es nicht nochmal vorkommt.

Offering solutions | Lösungen anbieten

We will replace the cards right away.	Wir werden die Karten umgehend ersetzen.
As a gesture of goodwill, this order will be free of charge.	Aus Kulanz schicken wir Ihnen eine kostenlose Ersatzlieferung.
We would also like to offer you a discount of 10% on your next order.	Außerdem möchten wir Ihnen einen Rabatt von 10% auf Ihre nächste Lieferung anbieten.

Ending the apology | Die Entschuldigung abschließen

We hope this solution is satisfactory for you.	Wir hoffen, dass diese Lösung für Sie zufriedenstellend ist.
We hope you are satisfied with this solution.	Wir hoffen, dass Sie mit dieser Lösung zufrieden sind.
I hope this helps.	Ich hoffe, dass Ihnen das hilft.

A–Z wordlist

A

abbreviation	Abkürzung
able, to be ~ to	fähig sein, im Stande sein
above	obige/r/s
above, the ~	das Obenstehende
according to	gemäß, nach
account	Konto
accounting	Buchhaltung
accounting system	Abrechnungssystem, Buchhaltungssystem
achievement	Leistung
activity	Maßnahmen, Aktivitäten
actually	eigentlich
to add	hinzufügen
advance, in ~	im Voraus
afraid, I'm ~ (that)	Leider …
agenda	Tagesordnung, Terminplan
ago, two days ~	vor zwei Tagen
to agree	zustimmen; vereinbaren
already	schon, bereits
amount	Betrag
to apologize (for sth.)	sich (für etw.) entschuldigen
apology	Entschuldigung
appointment	Termin
area	Gegend
around	circa, ungefähr
to arrange	ausmachen, vereinbaren
arrival	Ankunft
as soon as	sobald wie
as soon as possible (asap)	so schnell wie möglich, baldmöglichst
to ask for sth.	nach etw. fragen
to assist sb.	jdm. helfen
to attach	(an eine E-Mail) anhängen
attachment	Anhang
to attend	besuchen
attractive	ansprechend
to avoid	vermeiden

B

back and forth	hin und her
back, to be ~ at work	zurück auf der Arbeit sein
back, to get ~ to sb.	jdm. antworten
based in	mit Sitz in, ansässig in
because	weil, denn
because of	wegen, aufgrund
behind schedule	verspätet
below	unten
both	beide
bottle	Flasche
brochure	Broschüre, Prospekt
bullet point	Aufzählungspunkt
business cards	Visitenkarten
busy, to be ~	viel zu tun haben
busy times	Stoßzeiten
buyer	Einkäufer/in
by the way	übrigens

C

to call	anrufen; nennen
to cancel	absagen, stornieren
cancellation	Absage
capital letter	Großbuchstabe
cases, in urgent ~	in dringenden Fällen
to cause	verursachen
to cc (cc = carbon copy)	in Kopie an jdn. senden
CEO (Chief Executive Officer)	Geschäftsführer/in
chance	Gelegenheit
change	Veränderung, Änderung
to change	verändern
charge, free of ~	kostenlos
to check	überprüfen, (E-Mails:) abrufen
to check sth. out	etw. prüfen
to choose	(aus)wählen
to clarify	abklären, klarstellen
client	Kunde/Kundin, Auftraggeber/in
close	E-Mail: Schluss, Verabschiedung
close (adj.)	eng
to close an email	eine E-Mail beenden
colleague	Kollege, Kollegin
to collect	sammeln
come, sth. has ~ up	etw. ist dazwischen gekommen
comment	Kommentar
to complain	sich beschweren
complaint	Beschwerde
to complete	vervollständigen, ausfüllen
complicated	kompliziert
concerning	betreffend, bezüglich
to confirm	bestätigen, (Termin) zusagen
confusing	unübersichtlich, verwirrend
to connect	in Verbindung kommen
to contact	kontaktieren
contract	Vertrag
convenient	passend, günstig
convenient, to be ~ for sb.	jdm. passen
course	Kurs, Lehrgang
course, of ~	natürlich
crash	(Computer:) Absturz
CTO (Chief Technical Officer)	Technischer Vorstand
current(ly)	aktuell, gegenwärtig
customer	Kunde/Kundin

D

daily operations	Tagesgeschäft
data	Daten, Informationen, Angaben
date	Datum, private Verabredung
date, to set a ~	einen Termin festlegen
deadline	Frist
deadline, to meet a ~	eine Frist einhalten

to **decide**	entscheiden, sich einigen	to **get off**	aussteigen
decision	Entscheidung	to **get used to doing sth.**	sich daran gewöhnen, etw.
to **decline**	ablehnen		zu tun
delay	Verzögerung, Verspätung		
to **delete**	löschen	**glad ..., I'd be ~**	Gerne werde ich …
to **deliver**	liefern	**goodwill, as a gesture of ~**	aus Kulanz
delivery date	Liefertermin	**greeting**	Begrüßung, Anrede
demo equipment	Vorführgeräte		
demonstration, to give a ~	zeigen, vorführen, eine	**H**	
	Demonstration geben	to **have a baby**	ein Baby bekommen
		to **have a lot to do**	viel zu tun haben
department (dept.)	Abteilung	to **have no idea**	keine Ahnung haben
departure	Abreise	**head office**	Zentrale, Hauptsitz
to **describe**	beschreiben	**head technician**	leitende/r Techniker/in
description	Beschreibung	**headquarters**	Standort,
difference	Differenzbetrag		Hauptniederlassung
different	unterschiedlich, andere/r/s	to **hear back from sb.**	eine Antwort von jdm.
difficult	schwer, schwierig		bekommen, von jdm. hören
disappointed	enttäuscht	**helpful**	hilfreich
discount	Rabatt	**high priority**	sehr wichtig, hohe Priorität
to **discuss sth.**	über etw. sprechen	to **hire sb.**	jdn. einstellen
discussion	Gespräch, Diskussion	**honest**	ehrlich
draft	Entwurf	to **hope**	hoffen
due, to be ~	fällig sein	**HR (human resources)**	Personalabteilung
E		**I**	
effective	wirksam, effektiv	**idea, to have no ~**	keine Ahnung haben
either ... or ...	entweder … oder ….	to **ignore**	ignorieren, nicht beachten
emergency	Notfall	**illness**	Krankheit
especially	besonders, insbesondere,	**important**	wichtig, bedeutend
	vor allem	**impression**	Eindruck
even worse	noch schlimmer	**inbox**	Posteingang
evening	Abend	**including**	einschließlich, (mit)samt
every day	täglich	**in-company**	innerbetrieblich
exactly	genau, fehlerfrei	**inconvenience**	Unannehmlichkeiten
experience	Erfahrung (en)	**incorrect**	falsch, nicht richtig
to **explain**	erklären, darstellen	**information (info)**	Angaben, Information(en)
external	außerbetrieblich	**in-house**	innerbetrieblich
		to **inquire about sth.**	anfragen
F		**inquiry**	Anfrage
face to face	von Angesicht zu	to **install**	installieren, einbauen
	Angesicht, persönlich	**installation**	Montage; Einbau,
field	Bereich, Gebiet		Einrichtung
figures	Zahlen	**instant message (im)**	Sofortnachricht
final	letzte/r/s	**instead of**	anstatt, stattdessen
to **finish**	beenden, fertig sein	**interested**	interessiert
first name	Vorname	**interesting**	interessant
first of all	vor allem, erstens	to **introduce oneself**	sich vorstellen
folder	Ordner	**invitation**	Einladung
follow-up	Folge-, *(E-Mail:)* zweite	**invoice**	Rechnung
to **forget**	vergessen	**irrelevant**	unwichtig
formal	förmlich, formell		
to **forward**	weiterleiten	**J K**	
forward, to look ~ to sth.	sich auf etw. freuen	**just now**	eben jetzt, gerade jetzt
forward, to look ~	sich darauf freuen, etw. zu	to **keep**	halten
to doing sth.	tun	to **keep things short**	sich kurz fassen
free of charge	kostenlos	**key user**	Hauptnutzer/in
full	vollständig, ganz	**kitchen**	Teeküche, Küche
full of	voll mit, voller	to **know**	wissen, kennen
further	weitere	**know, to let sb. ~**	jdm. Bescheid geben
G		**L**	
general, in ~	im Allgemeinen, meistens	**large**	groß, umfangreich
gentle reminder	freundliche Erinnerung	**last but not least**	zu guter Letzt
gesture, as a ~ of goodwill	aus Kulanz	**last name**	Nachname
to **get back to sb.**	sich wieder bei jdm.	**latest, at the ~**	spätestens
	melden, jdm. antworten	**lazy**	faul

leader, team ~	Gruppenleiter/in, Teamleiter/in
to leave	abfahren, abfliegen; verlassen
to let sb. know	jdm. Bescheid geben
line	Linie, Reihe
logistics department	Logistikabteilung
to look forward to sth.	sich auf etw. freuen
to look forward to doing sth.	sich darauf freuen, etw. zu tun
to look into the matter	der Sache nachgehen

M

machinery	Maschinen
main	Haupt-; wichtigste/r/s
to make sure	versichern; dafür sorgen
manual	Handbuch, Betriebsanleitung
to mark	kennzeichnen
marketing	Vertrieb
matter, to look into the ~	der Sache nachgehen
to mean	bedeuten; meinen
to meet	treffen, kennenlernen
to meet a deadline	eine Frist einhalten
message	Nachricht
midday	Mittag
middle	Mitte
midnight	Mitternacht
minutes	Protokoll
to miss sth.	etw. verpassen
missing, to be ~	fehlen
mistake	Fehler
monthly	monatlich
motivated	motiviert
move	Umzug
to move	umziehen
to move sth.	etw. verschieben

N

nationality	Nationalität, Staatsangehörigkeit
native speaker	Muttersprachler/in
near	in der Nähe von
to need	brauchen, benötigen
news	Neuigkeiten, Nachrichten
noon (AE)	Mittag
notice, at short ~	kurzfristig

O

of course	natürlich
offer	Angebot
to offer	anbieten
Oh dear.	Ach je.
once	einmal
opening sentence	Eröffnungssatz
operation, in ~	in Betrieb
opposite	gegenüber
order	Bestellung, Auftrag
order, to place an ~	eine Bestellung aufgeben
to organize	organisieren
out of office message	Abwesenheitsnachricht
outbox	Postausgang
outcome	Ergebnis
outstanding	Rechnung: offen, noch nicht beglichen
to overcharge	zu viel berechnen

P

packaging	Verpackung
participant	Teilnehmer/in
payment	Bezahlung, Zahlung
to perform	funktionieren, arbeiten
period	Zeitraum, Dauer
personal(ly)	persönlich
personnel	Personal
pharma company	Pharma-Unternehmen
phone, by ~	telefonisch, am Telefon
to place an order	eine Bestellung aufgeben
planner	Planer/in
plant	Werk, Betrieb, Fabrik
polite	höflich
politeness	Höflichkeit
possible, as soon as ~ (asap)	so schnell wie möglich, baldmöglichst
to prefer	vorziehen
present	Geschenk
to present	präsentieren, zeigen
price list	Preisliste
pricing	Preisgestaltung
to print (out)	(aus)drucken
priority, high ~	sehr wichtig, hohe Priorität
to proceed	vorgehen
to process	bearbeiten
to produce	herstellen, produzieren
product line	Produktlinie, Sortiment
product specification	Produktbeschreibung
program	Programm
to purchase	kaufen, anschaffen
to put sb. in cc	jdn. in cc setzen, eine Mail in Kopie an jdn. senden

Q

quality assurance	Qualitätssicherung
quality test	Qualitätstest
questionnaire	Fragebogen
quick(ly)	schnell, prompt
quote, quotation	Angebot

R

range, a wide ~ of	eine breite Palette an
re	bezüglich, hinsichtlich
reason	Grund, Ursache
to receive	erhalten, bekommen
reception desk	Rezeption
to refer to sth.	auf etw. Bezug nehmen
to refund	erstatten
regarding	bezüglich, hinsichtlich
regular(ly)	regelmäßig
regulation	Vorschrift, Regel
to remember sb.	sich an jdn. erinnern
to remember to do sth.	daran denken, etw. zu tun
to remind sb. of sth.	jdn. an etw. erinnern
reminder	Erinnerung, Mahnung
reminder, gentle ~	freundliche Erinnerung
to repair sth.	etw. reparieren
to replace	ersetzen
reply	Antwort
to reply	antworten
report	Bericht
request	Anfrage, Bitte
to request	(an)fragen, anfordern, erbitten

requirements	Anforderungen, Bedarf
to **reread**	noch einmal lesen
research	Forschung
to **reserve**	reservieren
responsible, to **be ~ for sth.**	für etw. zuständig/ verantwortlich sein
result	Ergebnis
résumé	Lebenslauf
to **return**	zurückkommen
right away	sofort, schleunigst
risk, at ~	gefährdet
rule	Regel, Vorschrift

S
safety-	Sicherheits-
sales	Vertrieb, Verkauf
sales staff	Verkaufspersonal, Vertriebsmitarbeiter/innen
sample	Probestück, Muster
satisfactory	zufriedenstellend
satisfied	zufrieden
to **save time**	Zeit sparen
see, I ~.	Ich verstehe.
schedule, behind ~	verspätet
schedule, on ~	im Zeitplan
seldom	selten
to **send**	senden, schicken
sender	Absender/in
service	Dienstleistung, Service, Dienst
to **set a date**	einen Termin festlegen
to **set up**	arrangieren, einrichten
shift	Schicht
shipment	Lieferung, Versand
short form	Kurzform
short, at ~ notice	kurzfristig
to **sign up**	sich anmelden
similar	gleich, ähnlich
simple	einfach
solution	Lösung
to **solve**	lösen
sometimes	manchmal
to **sound**	klingen
specific	bestimmt, spezifisch
spreadsheet	(Kalkulations-)Tabelle
staff	Personal
statistics	Statistiken
status	Stand, Lage, Zustand
to **stay**	bleiben, wohnen, sich aufhalten
still	(immer) noch
structure	Struktur, Aufbau
subject (line)	Betreff(zeile)
to **suggest**	vorschlagen
suggestion	Vorschlag
to **summarize**	zusammenfassen
summary	Zusammenfassung
to **supply**	liefern
support	Hilfe, Unterstützung
Sure.	Natürlich./Sicherlich.
sure, to make ~	versichern, dafür sorgen
to **swap**	austauschen

T
to **take place**	stattfinden
team leader	Gruppenleiter/in, Teamleiter/in
technical	technisch
text (message)	SMS
though	aber, allerdings
time, on ~	pünktlich, rechtzeitig
times, at all ~	die ganze Zeit
tone	Tonfall
tone, the right ~	ein angemessener Ton
trade fair	Messe, Fachmesse
traffic light	Ampel
training	Einweisung, Schulung
training course	Schulung, Kurs
training session	Schulungseinheit
to **transfer (money)**	(Geld) überweisen
translator	Übersetzer/in
travel	Reise
trip	Reise
to **trust sb.**	jdm. vertrauen
type	Typ, Art
typos	Tippfehler

U V
unfortunately	leider
unsure	unsicher
up to date	aktuell
update	Lagebericht, Update
to **update sth.**	etw. aktualisieren
to **update sb.**	jdn. auf den neuesten Stand bringen, jdn. informieren
to **upload**	hochladen
urgent	dringend, eilig
urgent cases, in ~	in dringenden Fällen
to **use**	verwenden, benutzen
used, to get ~ to doing sth.	sich daran gewöhnen, etw. zu tun
useful	nützlich
user	Anwender/in, Nutzer/in
vacation	Urlaub, Ferien
video call	Videoanruf
to **visit sb.**	jdn. besuchen

W X Y Z
weak	schwach
whatever	egal welche
whether	ob
whole	ganze/r/s
wide	breit
to **win**	gewinnen
to **wish**	wünschen, wollen
to **work**	arbeiten; funktionieren
working times	Arbeitszeiten
writing, in ~	schriftlich
wrong	falsch
yet, not ... ~	noch nicht

Tracklist

Track	Unit	Exercise	Running time
01	Title/Copyright		0:50
02	Unit 1	Exercise 3	1:01
03	Unit 1	Exercise 8	1:18
04	Unit 2	Exercise 6	2:24
05	Unit 3	Exercise 9	1:45
06	Unit 4	Exercise 9	1:22
07	Unit 5	Exercise 7	1:50
08	Unit 6	Exercise 10	0:53
09	Unit 7	Exercise 9	2:03
10	Unit 8	Exercise 9	2:01
Total running time			15:27

Studio: Clarity Studio Berlin

Regie und Aufnahmeleitung: Christian Schmitz

Tontechnik: Christian Marx

Sprecher/innen: Tania Carlin, Malgorzata Dudley, Steve Ellery, Marianne Graffam, Jeffrey Mittleman, Helena Prince, Justin Reddig, Dharmander Singh, Ian Smith, Tomas Sinclair Spencer, Simon Srebrny, Clare Wigfall